HEROES *of* **AMERICA**™

George Washington

by **Marian Leighton**

illustrations by **Martin Salvador**

BARONET
BOOKS

BARONET BOOKS, New York, New York

HEROES OF AMERICA™

Edited by
Joshua Hanft and Rochelle Larkin

HEROES OF AMERICA™ is a series of dramatized lives of great Americans especially written for younger readers. We have selected men and women whose accomplishments and achievements can inspire children to set high goals for themselves and work with all of us for a better tomorrow.

Table of Contents

Important Dates

1732 George Washington born in Virginia

1749 Appointed to first public office: surveyor
     of Culpeper County

1756 Appointed commander-in-chief of
     Virginia Militia

1759 Married Martha Dandridge Custis

1759 Elected to Virginia House of Burgesses

1774 Served as delegate to Continental
     Congress

1775 Named commander-in-chief of the
     Continental Army

1781 Accepted the surrender of Lord
     Cornwallis

1783 Retired from the army to return to
     Mount Vernon

1787 Presided over the Federal Constitutional
     Convention

1789 Took office as first president of United
     States of America

1793 Unanimously elected to second term
     as president

1796 Delivered Farewell Address

1799 George Washington died and was
     buried at Mount Vernon

Chapter 1

A Virginia Boyhood

"Hang on, George! Hang on there, boy!" Lawrence Washington shouted. The young man was sitting on a fence, watching his little seven-year-old half-brother as the youngster bucked and bounced in the saddle of the unbroken horse he had determined to train by himself.

George bit his lip, clutching at the reins. He forced his long, strong legs around the horse's flank, digging his heels into the underbelly and holding on for dear life. He was very strong for a seven year old.

George Clutched at the Reins.

because even for wealthy families like the Washingtons who had slaves to do most of their work for them, life in colonial America was hard and active, and lived mainly in the rugged outdoors.

It was more than two hours since George had thrown his saddle over the horse's back, and still the animal struggled with all its might, trying to throw its young rider. But George was even more determined. He had announced that he would break this headstrong animal, and break it he would.

Suddenly, the horse dropped to the ground. Its knees buckled as it went down. George sprang away quickly to keep from being thrown, or worse, crushed underneath.

Lawrence jumped down from the fence and raced across the pasture. "George, are you all right?" he asked, kneeling down to where the young rider was sprawled on the grass. "What happened?"

"He didn't throw me," George answered defiantly.

7

"I jumped when I felt him going down." George rubbed his scraped elbows and knees.

"Why did he do that, I wonder?" Lawrence muttered. Satisfied that George wasn't seriously hurt himself, Lawrence turned his attention to the horse.

The large animal groaned and turned its head aside.

"He's dead!" Lawrence said in amazement, almost to himself. He turned back to his half-brother. "He just gave up!" he said. "But you didn't—did you, George?"

George tried to smile, but he was still hurting a little too much for that. "No, I didn't," he said proudly. "I never give up."

Lawrence smiled at those words. He squeezed his stepbrother's shoulder playfully. Although Lawrence was fifteen years older and one of the sons of their father's first marriage, he and George were great friends.

The Horse Turned Its Head Aside.

GEORGE WASHINGTON

George liked nothing more than to stay at Lawrence's estate, Epsewasson. It was both an escape from the constant gaze of his mother, Mary, and a wonderful place for a boy to grow up.

There were deep forests to wander in, to look for animals who made their homes in and under the thickly growing trees. There were meadows for catching insects in, small brooks and the great Potomac River to fish in, horses and dogs and farm-yard creatures for pets. For George, Epsewasson was his home away from home, and very nearly heaven on earth.

In later life, when it indeed became George's home, it was known as Mount Vernon. Today it is a landmark for all Americans.

For now, though, home for George was the family farm, big enough to be considered a plantation, near a town called Fredericksberg. The town was where he went to school. Home was called Ferry Farm.

GEORGE WASHINGTON

It was home not only to George, of course, but to his parents, Mary and Augustine, and George's three younger brothers and sister Elizabeth. George's other older half-brother, Austin, was in school in England at this time.

England was where the Washington family had come from, to this great new wilderness of Virginia. Virginia was a colony of England's, ruled by what the colonists called the "mother country." George's great-grandfather, John Washington, had been the first of their line to make the dangerous ocean voyage to this new world.

George's grandfather and father had been born here, as had George himself, though no one knows exactly when.

The Washington family Bible lists George's birthdate as February 11, 1731. But a great change was made in the calendar when George was about twenty years old. When the calendar changed, the

George Did Well at His Lessons.

date of his birthday became February 22, 1732!

Just as England, the mother country, ruled the thirteen colonies, Mary Washington ruled the family at Ferry Farm. Although George was her oldest child, she treated him more like a baby than she did the younger ones. Maybe it was just that she worried about him more, but George didn't see it that way. To him, it was a never-ending battle between what he wanted to do and what his mother would allow.

Even school was easier than their constant squabbles. George did well at his lessons. His teacher, the Reverend Mr. James Marye, taught the dozen or so children in his charge the sort of practical things they would need to know as grown-ups in the New World.

But at the same time, the teacher wanted them to behave like future ladies and gentlemen. Lessons in conduct were very important, and George learned rules of cleanliness and behavior that stayed with him all his life.

It was by memorizing proverbs, or sayings, that children were taught in those days. One of the ideas that stayed with George was "undertake not what you cannot perform, but be careful to keep your promise."

George paid a lot of attention to this, and to all of his lessons. He studied very hard and worked on his lessons until they were perfect.

Even his three playful little brothers could not distract him. His studies soon became more important than playing. He often seemed lonely even in the midst of a big and active family.

George was ready to read the books in Lawrence's large library. But now something serious interfered. Lawrence had to leave Epsewasson to join the army. George was very proud of his older brother. He thought Lawrence was a hero, but he was worried.

His Three Playful Little Brothers

Lawrence might be injured or killed, because Great
Britain, as England is also called, had declared war
on Spain.

It was known as "The War of Jenkins's Ear."
What a strange name for a war, George thought. It
started because Spain had colonies in Central and
South America, just as England did in North America. The Spanish Coastguard tried to stop British
ships from trading with the Spanish colonies and
taking profits that Spain wanted all for herself. The
war got its name when a Spanish coastguardsman
cut off the ear of a British sea captain named Robert
Jenkins.

The British army recruited an American regiment for an attack on Cartagena, a port in Colombia, South America. The city was rumored to be a
storehouse of Spanish treasure.

"I have been commissioned as an officer of the
American Regiment!" Lawrence announced to his

family. "My men will sail from Chesapeake Bay to join Admiral Vernon's fleet in Jamaica. From there, it's on to Colombia."

"We will pray for your safety, of course," said Augustine Washington. "But I wish you would change your mind and stay out of the war."

"Please don't go!" pleaded George, hugging his brother with all his might, as if holding him very tightly would prevent him from leaving.

Disaster, not treasure, awaited the British army at Cartagena.

"There's been a terrible defeat!" said the sailors in Fredericksburg returning from the British West Indies with the latest news. "The British army lost a great number of fighters!"

And the American Regiment? Nobody knew. Many weeks passed before a letter arrived at Ferry Farm. Was it a notice of Lawrence's death? Augustine Washington's hand trembled so much as he

"Hooray!" George Shouted.

unsealed the envelope that he didn't even notice that the address was in Lawrence's handwriting.

The Regiment is being disbanded now. I'll be home soon, Lawrence wrote.

"Hooray!" George shouted. He had feared that he might never see his beloved half-brother again.

There was a double homecoming for the Washington family. Lawrence returned from the war, and Austin came home from school in London. It was wonderful for the whole family to be reunited. They sat around the dinner table and talked for hours. Lawrence told them about the war, and Austin talked about Appleby, his English school. George hoped to go to both the army and to Appleby when he got older.

"I have some news too!" George's father announced. "I read in the *Virginia Gazette* that Colonel William Fairfax, one of the richest and most important men in the colony of Virginia, has just bought the land next to Epsewasson!"

"By the way," Lawrence announced, "I have decided to change the name of my plantation from Epsewasson to Mount Vernon, in honor of Admiral Vernon."

While the elder Washingtons kept track of all the new settlers in the colony of Virginia, George concentrated on his schoolwork. He studied geography, history, Greek and Latin, but his favorite subject was math.

"Look what I found!" George said to his father one evening. They were looking through some of the things in the storage sheds on Ferry Farm. He held up a compass, a ruler, and lots of other things that he couldn't identify.

"Those are my surveying tools," Augustine Washington replied. "They are used to measure a plot of land and draw a map with boundaries. If you buy land, you can write in the deed exactly how many

He Held Up a Compass.

acres it contains and where it begins and ends."

"There are so many tools!" George said. "Is it difficult to be a land surveyor?"

"Not really," his father answered. " You just have to do some mathematical calculations. By the time you finish school, you should know enough math to be able to do the job."

"I think that would be a very interesting profession," George declared. But history had a far different career in store for George Washington.

Chapter 2

Growing Pains

After Lawrence returned from the war, he became a very important and well-known official in the Virginia colony. He was appointed Adjutant of Virginia because of his military experience. The adjutant was in charge of commanding the military units, called militia. They defended the colony.

Besides serving as adjutant, Lawrence was busy with Mount Vernon and courting Colonel William Fairfax's daughter, Nancy. He had less and less time left to spend with his younger brother, but George

George Played with His Cousins.

wasn't angry. The times they spent together were still special. When he couldn't visit Lawrence, George played with his cousins who lived further south along the Potomac River in an area called Chotank.

"Samson, please take me to Chotank today!" he would tell the slave who always accompanied him on the ride. George always said "please," even though a slave had no choice but to obey a member of his master's family.

When George climbed down from his horse, Samson went back to Ferry Farm. George and his cousins played follow-the-leader, flew kites, pitched quoits, raced across the meadows, did cartwheels on the grass, played ball and games like badminton, lotto, and loo. George loved to remain overnight, staying up late, laughing and whispering.

One day in the spring of 1743, George arrived at Chotank and joined his cousins on the lawn. Hardly had they begun to play when Samson returned. "Surely you haven't come to fetch me yet!" cried George. "I just got here!"

The expression on Samson's face indicated he was bringing bad news. "Your father is very sick. You are to come home immediately."

The house at Ferry Farm was usually full of children's voices and family activities, but that day, all was quiet. George's younger sister and brothers huddled together in frightened silence. His mother struggled to hold back tears. Lawrence and Austin paced the floor, shaking their heads.

"Mr. Washington is suffering from gout of the stomach," the doctor said. "I'm afraid there is no hope for his recovery."

In those days, there were a lot of illnesses that doctors couldn't treat and often couldn't even identify. "Gout of the stomach" could have meant anything from a heart attack to a burst appendix.

"Your Father Is Very Sick."

Augustine Washington had signed his will and said his prayers. Before long his body was buried in the Washington family cemetery.

"It is so strange to walk into the living room and not see father sitting in his favorite chair next to the fire and reading the *Virginia Gazette*," George said to Lawrence. "I always wanted to spend more time with him, but the the plantation and his other work kept him so busy. Now I'll never have the chance."

Lawrence tried to spend more time with George, but he had many new responsibilities now that Augustine was gone. Since Lawrence was the eldest son, he inherited most of the Washington family's lands along the Potomac River. The only person who seemed to have lots of time for George was his mother—but Mary's constant attention bothered rather than soothed him.

"What are you doing?" she would ask, or, "Where are you going? And when will you be back?"

With her husband gone, Mary clung to her first-born son. She just couldn't stop worrying about him.

"George, it's such a hot day, don't you want a mug of cold cider?" she would say, or, "It's awfully cold. You must put on your coat!"

George was eleven years old when his father died. He was almost as old as Lawrence and Austin had been when they entered Appleby. George had heard so much about the school from his half-brothers that he longed to go there. But what would his mother say? Finally he found the courage to ask her.

"It's bad enough that you want to take the ferry to Fredericksburg alone!" she replied. "And now you want to sail all the way to England? No!"

"But, Mother—I can take care of myself. There's nothing for you to worry about. Look how big and strong I am already. No one can beat me at wrestling and I can throw a ball or an iron bar farther than most men can!"

Mary Washington's Mind Was Set.

GEORGE WASHINGTON

"George, the answer is still no!" his mother said sternly.

The next time George brought up the subject of Appleby, Mary Washington had another reason not to let him go. "Now that your father is dead, we have to save our money, George," she told him. "We can't afford the cost of Appleby."

"That's not true," Lawrence declared. "Father left the family plenty of money, and the land we own is worth even more." But Mary Washington's mind was set. George was to stay close to home.

"Surely you can get as much education as you need right here in Virginia!" Mary declared.

George's formal schooling never went much beyond the elementary grades, even though he was very intelligent. He had a practical outlook on life, and learned new skills very quickly on his own.

George stopped going to school when he was fourteen. He decided that he had learned everything that the Reverend Mr. Marye could teach him. He could always study on his own if he wanted to learn more. Meanwhile, he could spend more time with Lawrence at Mount Vernon where his mother couldn't fuss over him.

Soon after the death of Augustine Washington, the Washington family had a happy occasion to celebrate. George was the first to know.

"I have some wonderful news!" Lawrence told him one evening during one of George's frequent visits to Mount Vernon. "I'm going to marry Nancy Fairfax."

"That means we'll hardly ever see each other!" George complained without thinking. He quickly bit his tongue. "Please forgive me, Lawrence. I do want you to be happy. But I hope you'll save some time for me!"

"Of course I will. In fact, all the important people in Virginia will be coming to Mount Vernon. We'll have elegant parties, foxhunts, and all kinds of

He Could Always Study on His Own.

other activities. I'll always want you to join us."

The step-brothers embraced joyfully. They were still exceedingly fond of each other. The wedding took place at Belvoir, the mansion that the Fairfaxes had built next to Mount Vernon.

Lawrence kept his word. He invited George to his home often. Colonel Fairfax also took a liking to George and talked to him about many interesting things. By the time George was fifteen years old, he was part of the exciting social life at Mount Vernon.

A tall, muscular young man with good manners, George made an excellent impression on the Fairfax family. He was an accomplished horseback rider and hunter. He also knew how to listen politely to the endless discussions about land that went on among Lawrence and his relatives and friends. All of them wanted to expand their landholdings.

George hoped to acquire some land of his own. "I'm glad that you're getting so rich," he told

Lawrence. "I only wish I had enough money to buy some good land!"

"According to Father's will, Ferry Farm will be yours on your twenty-first birthday," Lawrence replied.

"I know," said George. "And the crops on the farm will bring in enough for me to live on, but they'll never make me rich! And besides, what shall I do in the meantime? I'm only fifteen!"

Lawrence had given a lot of thought to George's future. He couldn't imagine his restless younger brother finding happiness in the management of Ferry Farm, especially if he had to continue living with his quarrelsome mother.

"How would you like to go to sea?" Lawrence asked.

"I'd like that!" George replied enthusiastically. "I could be a midshipman in the Royal Navy and some-day become an admiral like Edward Vernon."

"You'll Have to Get Mother's Permission."

"That would be nice," said Lawrence, "but unfortunately the British Navy prefers native-born Englishmen rather than colonists. I was thinking that you could sign on as a cabin boy on a merchant ship. You could work your way up to second mate, then first mate, and finally to captain. As a captain, you would own your ship and make a good profit on all the cargoes it carries."

George didn't really care what his title was, so long as he could take exciting voyages to London, the West Indies, and everywhere else in the world.

"There's just one problem," Lawrence said, interrupting George's daydream. "You will have to get your mother's permission to become a cabin boy."

George's spirits had soared; now he returned abruptly to earth. "She'll never let me go! She still treats me like a two-year-old!" he groaned.

Mary Washington had actually become more lenient since George was in his teens. But she was still quite stubborn, and besides, it was hard to tell what she was thinking. As soon as he returned to Ferry Farm from Mount Vernon, George brought up the idea.

"Going to sea doesn't sound very good to me," his mother said. "But I'll think about it."

Weeks passed, and she continued to think. George grew tired of waiting for an answer. He appealed to Lawrence for help. Shortly afterward, a messenger arrived from Mount Vernon to Ferry Farm with a letter to Mary Washington. It was from Lawrence, and it contained a long list of reasons why George should be allowed to go to sea. But Mary still wasn't convinced. She wanted to think a while longer.

More weeks passed. George kept bringing up the issue, but with no success. At last, Mary Washington summoned her son.

"I've written a letter to your Uncle Joseph," she

A Long List of Reasons

told George. Uncle Joseph was Joseph Ball, Mary Washington's half-brother.

"I've always trusted your uncle's judgment in matters such as this. Surely he'll be able to advise us whether or not you should go to sea," Mary went on. "When I hear from him, then certainly I'll be able to give you my answer, George."

Six more months passed before Joseph Ball's reply to Mary Washington's letter arrived, and the advice he offered meant disappointment for George.

Sailors aren't well paid or well treated, Uncle Joseph wrote. Even if George became master of his own ship, the letter went on, he would be unlikely to get rich. He would make more money as a planter, even if he only owned a few acres of land. *Better yet,* Uncle Joseph wrote, *he should be made an apprentice to a tinker.*

"The sons of gentlemen don't take jobs fixing kettles and pots!" George told his mother angrily when she had relayed what Uncle Joseph had written. "I would much rather become an apprentice to a surveyor. I'm sure that Lawrence or Colonel Fairfax could arrange that."

George went immediately to the Ferry Farm sheds, where his father's old surveyors' tools were stored. He spent the next few months learning to measure land and draw maps. He worked at the side of a master surveyor and practiced his new skills by making surveys of Lawrence's turnip patch and Austin's orchards.

George greatly enjoyed this work. It let him use the math skills he had mastered in school. He liked working outdoors, as well as escaping for long periods of time from his still-strict mother. Now, instead of just listening while Lawrence and the Fairfaxes talked about land, George could participate in the discussions and contribute ideas of his own.

In the summer of 1747, there was an exciting new

George Memorized "Rules of Civility"

topic of conversation. "Lord Thomas Fairfax is coming from England!" Lawrence told George. "He will stay with the colonel at Belvoir."

"I can't wait to meet him!" exclaimed George. "I've never met a real lord! I hope I make a good impression on him!"

George found a book called *Youth's Behavior* and studied it carefully. The book contained "Rules of Civility" that George memorized. He felt that there was nothing more awful than making a fool of yourself in public.

George tried to imagine what an English nobleman would be like. Probably he would be very dignified and wear clothes cut in the latest London fashion. George feared that his own best coat and breeches, or knee-length pants, would look shabby next to Lord Fairfax's, but at least he would have perfect manners. He knew that he must not spit in the fire, pick his teeth, or forget to stand up when

His Lordship entered the room.

George counted the days until Lord Fairfax arrived. At last, Lawrence announced that it was time. They set out from Mount Vernon for the mansion at Belvoir.

"Come in and let me introduce you to our honorable guest from London!" Colonel Fairfax greeted them at the door.

George was shocked! To him, Lord Fairfax looked more like a farmer or a woodsman than an English gentleman. His clothes were old and rumpled and dirty. His face was unwashed, and his hair uncombed. And his manners were terrible!

"If Lord Fairfax ever read the Rules of Civility, he certainly didn't follow them," George remarked to Lawrence when they were back at Mount Vernon. "He was rude to most of the men and refused even to talk to the women. And if he has a wardrobe like noblemen are supposed to have, he must not have

George Was Shocked!

bothered to bring it to America."

"I guess he's not the nicest houseguest one would wish for," Lawrence admitted, "but Colonel Fairfax can't complain. He became rich only because His Lordship let him serve as his land agent in Virginia."

Indeed, Lord Fairfax could think about nothing but his land. He spent almost all of his time in the colonel's library, studying maps of his extensive properties and plotting strategies for selling them at the best prices possible.

Virginia was growing rapidly, and each new wave of settlers that came had to go farther inland to find property for farms and homes. There was already settlement in the foothills of the Blue Ridge Mountains. Soon people would cross the mountains and move westward into the Shenandoah Valley. That valley was becoming the most desirable place to buy land. There were millions of acres ready to be cleared and farmed. But who had the right to sell this valuable land?

"The entire valley belongs to the King of England!" declared the Royal Governor of Virginia.

"No!" argued Lord Thomas Fairfax, Colonel Fairfax's cousin. "That land is mine!"

The dispute was referred to His Majesty's Privy Council in London. Luckily for the Fairfax family and for Lawrence Washington, Colonel Fairfax's son-in-law—the Council ruled in favor of Lord Fairfax. In fact, the Council determined that the Fairfaxes owned not only the Shenandoah Valley, but also an entire section of the Allegheny Mountains extending into what is now the state of West Virginia. There were five million acres in all!

There was great excitement at Mount Vernon and Belvoir when the news came. The Fairfax family was about to become richer than ever. Lawrence Washington could now buy land in the Shenandoah

"To Cross the Blue Ridge Mountains."

Valley and sell at a handsome profit.

"The land must be surveyed immediately. How would you like to join a surveying party?" Lord Fairfax asked George one day.

"What kind of party is that?" George replied.

"Much different from the kind of parties we have at Mount Vernon," Lord Fairfax laughed. "We're going to cross the Blue Ridge Mountains into the Shenandoah Valley and divide the land there into farm-size lots. Then we can sell the lots to people who want to settle there."

George could hardly wait to go, especially since George William Fairfax, Lawrence's brother-in-law, was a member of the party. George William was seven years older than George, but the two had become close friends.

"I suppose you should ask your mother's permission to go on this trip, even though you're sixteen and almost a full-grown man," Lawrence reminded

George. "I shall send a messenger to her."

To George's great relief, Mary Washington said yes.

At last! George could take his place with the other men going out into the wilderness and seeing more of the country than he ever had before. It was a trip not only away from his mother, but from the whole routine of his life. This would be his first great adventure.

"I Shall Send a Messenger."

Chapter 3

An Adventurous Career

George was happier than ever that he had chosen land surveying as his profession. Surveyors were very important people in colonial Virginia. They played a major role in opening up the vast new lands that lay to the west of the original thirteen American colonies.

"Get ready for the greatest adventure of your life!" George William Fairfax said. "Life in the wilderness is nothing like life at Ferry Farm and Mount Vernon. Back home the slaves do everything. Now you'll be lucky even to have shelter at night. Most likely you'll have to sleep in the woods. And remember—there are bears and rattlesnakes there!"

"I've had plenty of soft living. Now I want to be tough and learn how to take care of myself," George replied.

George survived the hard trip extremely well. During thirty-three days in the wilds of the Shenandoah Valley, he never complained. He slept outdoors on the bare ground and cooked his own meals over a campfire. One night a farmer invited the group of surveyors to spend the night in his house, but they had to sleep on straw mats full of bedbugs and fleas! And when he served them breakfast, there was no silverware.

Surveying the land was very difficult. The forests were so thick that it was impossible to make exact measurements, and the paths were so rocky that the horses often stumbled and nearly threw their riders.

"Strange People Out There"

To make matters worse, it rained almost every day. The surveyors had to work in wet clothes and muddy boots. But George enjoyed the work, and he earned a good amount of money for that time.

"It was certainly different," George told Lawrence when he returned to Belvoir. "There were some strange people out there—pioneers with thick beards, and shirts made from deerskin. They tell time by the sun. There were settlers from Germany who couldn't speak a word of English, trappers who caught animals in order to sell their fur, and Indians in war paint and feathers. And some of them even had human hair strung around their waists!"

"That must have frightened you!" Lawrence laughed.

"Luckily, the Indians turned out to be friendlier than they looked," George replied. "In fact, they showed us their war dances, and we smoked peace pipes together."

"It's good that you learned something about the tribes," Lawrence said. "But most important, I hear you did a very good job surveying the Shenandoah land."

Indeed, the head of the survey team had high praise for George. "You performed your duties extremely well on your first trip to the wilderness, George," he said. "I believe you're ready to earn a living as a land surveyor. And it's a very honorable profession, if I do say so myself!"

George took a short course at William and Mary College in Williamsburg, Virginia. He passed the test and got an official surveyor's license. But in addition to surveying land, he wished to purchase some land for himself. He could see that in five or ten years the Shenandoah Valley would change from wilderness to settled area, with farmhouses instead of log cabins, roads instead of trails, and plowed fields instead of meadows and forests.

The Head of the Team Had High Praise.

Great changes had already occurred in the area where George grew up. When his parents had moved to Ferry Farm on the upper Potomac River, the area was still mostly unsettled. By 1744, it had so many people it had become a county named Fairfax.

George was hired by the Fairfax County surveyor to help lay out the streets and measure the lots for the houses and other buildings in the county's first town, which came to be called Alexandria. His survey maps of Alexandria were so good that he became the chief surveyor of Culpeper County. It was about 30 miles from Fredericksburg, where he had gone by ferry as a child. In addition to this job, George was hired by Lord Fairfax to survey more land in the Shenandoah Valley. At the age of 18, George already had a successful career.

George's second trip to the wilderness was not nearly so enjoyable as his first. For one thing, he had to go alone. For another, he made the journey in the winter. The weather was so cold and damp that no matter how close to the fire he slept in his bearskin blanket, he couldn't get warm. The only thing that made the trip worthwhile was the large sum of money he made.

George William Fairfax greeted George on his return and introduced him to his new bride, Sally. George was shy with women, but Sally was so friendly that he felt at ease right away. He hoped that someday he might find a wife as pretty and charming as Sally.

Both George William and Lawrence were members of the House of Burgesses, the body of elected delegates that made Virginia's laws. Lawrence missed many of the sessions that winter because of an illness that wouldn't go away. He often felt too weak to leave Mount Vernon. Finally, when summer came, he was well enough to travel to London on

George Earned Money as a Surveyor.

business. Even the doctors there could not figure out what was wrong with him or how to cure him. In fact Lawrence had tuberculosis, a very serious disease.

Lawrence had better luck with his business deal. The king of England granted him 200,000 acres of land in Ohio to develop and sell. The king wanted settlements and forts there so that the French would not be able to seize the Ohio region. The British and French were rivals in a struggle to claim lands in North America.

George Washington earned a good deal of money in his job as surveyor of Culpeper County. He saved enough to buy three large tracts of land in the Shenandoah Valley. He also looked forward to surveying the land in Ohio that now belonged to Lawrence.

George not only worked hard; he also played hard. He attended parties, picnics, barbecues and dances. He and Lawrence went fox-hunting with the Fairfaxes or duck hunting in the marshes along the Potomac. George also spent time with his younger brothers. They liked to go to horse races or play cards and billiards in the taverns of Fredericksburg.

Spending time with the Fairfax family gave George an education that he could never have got at school. The Fairfaxes had a long tradition of defending individual liberty and freedom, and rebelling against the English kings who exercised absolute power.

The Fairfaxes and other members of the English land-owning class found their inspiration in the famous men of the ancient republic of Rome. These men were well-known for their morals and courage. They also had a strong sense of duty, honor, and service to their country.

The Fairfaxes put on amateur performances of plays from the Roman period that reflected these

They Went Duck Hunting in the Marshes.

ideas. George participated actively in these home theatricals. His favorite drama was *Cato*, the story of a man who sacrificed many of life's comforts to seek personal perfection. Such ideas had a powerful influence on George Washington, who was guided by them in his daily life.

During his late teenage years, George was very worried about Lawrence's health. His big brother felt fine during the summer, but during cold weather his illness returned. His doctor told him to spend the next winter in a warmer climate. Lawrence decided to sail to the island of Barbados. Since he was too weak to travel alone and Nancy didn't want to take their new baby to a strange place, George went with him. The time away from his job as a surveyor meant a loss of money, but Lawrence's health was more important to him than anything else.

The voyage to Barbados took more than a month.

GEORGE WASHINGTON

George was bored with the lack of activity on the ship. When they finally arrived, he lost no time exploring the island. There were lovely white houses, fields of pineapple and sugar cane, and gardens full of tropical flowers, but most of all George enjoyed seeing the fort that the British had built to defend Barbados from enemy attack.

Lawrence's health began to improve, but then George caught a dreadful disease called smallpox and nearly died. Today there are vaccinations to protect people from smallpox, but during George Washington's lifetime, many people got the disease, and many died. The high fever, terrible headaches and blisters all over his body made George miserable.

After George recovered, Lawrence told him to return to Virginia. George didn't want to leave his brother, but Lawrence seemed able to manage alone.

When George landed in America, he delivered some letters from people in Barbados to Virginia's

Dining at the Governor's Mansion

new Royal Governor, Robert Dinwiddie. He and the governor discovered many common interests, especially since Mr. Dinwiddie was also a land surveyor. George was honored to be invited to dine at the governor's mansion.

George began to worry again about Lawrence. A doctor had finally diagnosed his illness, but there was no cure. Lawrence's letters sounded more and more discouraging. Then, one day in June, a ship docked in the Potomac off Mount Vernon, and Lawrence staggered weakly to shore. His body was wasted, and his voice was barely above a whisper. George knew that his brother had come home to die.

George was 20 when Lawrence passed away. Since the death of Augustine Washington, George had become even more attached to Lawrence, who was like a father to him. His brother's death was a great loss not only to his family but to the colony of Virginia, where he had played a leading role.

Lawrence left Mount Vernon to his wife, but George was named as executor of the will, a position that put him in charge of Lawrence's business and financial affairs. George missed him terribly. He wanted to carry out his duties in a way that would have made Lawrence proud.

George unquestioningly assumed Lawrence's role as head of the Washington family. Although he was barely out of his teens, George was extraordinarily mature. At six feet, two inches tall and broad shouldered, a giant compared to most men of his time, he was both sensible and ambitious. Carrying out Lawrence's responsibilities at Mount Vernon, George took over management of the plantation.

George also wanted to follow in Lawrence's footsteps in public life. His chief goal was to fill his brother's position as Adjutant General of Virginia. Although only twenty years old and with no military experience, George wrote to Governor Dinwiddie to

At 6'2", Barely Out of His Teens

propose himself as Lawrence's replacement.

Instead of appointing a single individual to replace Lawrence, the governor planned to divide the colony of Virginia into three militia districts and select an adjutant for each. All three men he intended to choose were much older than George and had lots of experience. George, however, was determined to play a leading role in colonial affairs. Therefore, when the governor didn't reply to George's letter, he wrote a second time. His persistence brought success. In addition to appointing the three adjutants that he had in mind, Governor Dinwiddie created a fourth militia district, which covered the counties in southern Virginia. And he named George Washington as the adjutant for this district.

"Why not give the boy a chance?" said the governor to his aides, who expressed great surprise at his choice. "He is certainly persistent. And he wants so badly to be like his brother. I spent an evening with George, and he seems to be a fine young man."

On February 1,1753, only a few weeks before his twenty first birthday, George Washington took his oath of office. He wore a new uniform of red breeches and dark blue coat with brass buttons. A sword with a silver handle was strapped to his waist. George's new title was Major Washington.

As adjutant, George stood ready to train the militia from southern Virginia. Perhaps one day he would have to lead the militiamen into combat against an invasion across the frontier or as part of the British-French struggle for control of North America. Whatever the future might hold, young Major Washington was ready to do his duty.

One day, Governor Dinwiddie summoned George to his office.

"There is trouble in the Ohio Valley," the governor said. "French soldiers have been coming down the

"This Will Be A Dangerous Mission."

Ohio River from Canada. They have built a fort in English territory, south of Lake Erie. They have made alliances with several Indian tribes and are attacking English settlers. We must make sure that the Ohio territory remains in British hands and that our people there can live in peace."

"I shall take a message to the French ordering them to abandon their fort and warning them to stay off English land," George offered.

"This will be a dangerous mission," the governor warned. "The Ohio Valley is a thousand miles away. The journey will be full of hazards. But you have a well-earned reputation for courage and skill. If anyone can carry out this task, it is you."

"I shall be honored to serve you," Washington replied. "I'll find guides and interpreters and leave for Ohio at once!"

Chapter 4

A Wilderness Journey

Deep in the Ohio wilderness, George Washington's small party encountered many dangers. Hostile Indians surrounded and threatened them. Despite their compasses, which gave them a sense of direction, they lost their way on more than one occasion. There were no maps to guide them. The winter weather was so severe that streams froze, making drinking water difficult to find.

George Washington's greatest challenge on this dangerous journey was to cross the icy Allegheny

Severe Winter Weather Froze the Streams.

River safely. The party was on the last leg of its mission. They had reached a point on the Allegheny River where the city of Pittsburgh, Pennsylvania, is now located. George Washington, the young volunteer, and Christopher Gist, a veteran frontiersman twice his age, left the other members of the expedition and the slow-moving pack horses and went on ahead to search for a place to cross the river.

Large chunks of ice dotted the river and the water flowed very swiftly. Chopping down trees with a single small hatchet, George Washington and Christopher Gist fashioned logs into a raft. It was sundown when they climbed onto their freshly made transport.

"We'll never make it!" Gist moaned, as the dark violent currents of the river smashed against the raft. "We're sure to capsize!"

"Hold on and pray!" George shouted, trying to make himself heard above the roaring waters.

GEORGE WASHINGTON

Using every ounce of his great strength, George Washington shoved his pole straight down into the bottom of the raft, hoping to steady it until an opening appeared in the thundering stream of icy water. But the river was much too powerful even for a giant of a man like Washington. The raft spun in a circle out of control and pitched him head first into the freezing current.

"Oh, no!" Gist screamed in horror as the raft hurtled on downstream. Then George's long arm shot up above the water, and his hand grasped a protruding log. He barely managed to drag himself back aboard the raft.

But the two men were utterly stranded in the middle of the raging river. The temperature was well below freezing, and George Washington was soaked to the bone. Suddenly, in the distance, he spotted a little island.

"Try to pole the raft over there," he told Gist. "At

"We Can Walk Across!"

least it's a spot of dry land."

"I...don't know...if I can...make it!" Gist gasped. He was still paralyzed with fright at Washington's near-drowning, and his own fingers were frostbitten. Somehow they finally reached the island, and the two men stumbled ashore.

"This place is completely barren. There's not even a tree to chop down for firewood!" George said in dismay.

"We must keep walking back and forth to avoid freezing to death!" his comrade answered.

The night was frigid, but the dawn brought hope. "Look at the river, Chris!" George shouted joyously. "It's completely frozen! We don't need the raft anymore. We can just walk across!"

When they reached the other side, the two men slumped down on the frozen ground. George sat at the foot of a tree to recover from his exhaustion. A group of French soldiers passed by. Without revealing his identity or his reason for being in the wilderness, George Washington engaged them in conversation. Soon the French began drinking wine and offered some to the strangers. Washington and Gist drank only enough to be polite and then waited until the French became thoroughly drunk and began chattering about their troop movements and plans.

They told me it was their absolute design to take possession of the Ohio Valley and, by God, they would do it, George later wrote in his journal.

After the French soldiers moved on, Washington and Gist encountered a Native American chieftain named Halfking. Gist, who knew how to communicate with Native Americans, explained their mission, and George drew upon his previous experience with them to make Halfking feel at ease.

"Follow me," the chieftain motioned to the two. Then he summoned his braves, and together they

The French Began Chattering.

led the white men along hidden trails until they came to some log cabins surrounded by a heavy wooden fence. "This is the French fort," Halfking whispered.

The French commander, a dignified-looking elderly gentleman, received Washington but steadfastly refused his demands. "This land belongs to us, not to the English!" he insisted.

Although the Frenchman stood firm, Halfking admired George Washington's courage in confronting him. In fact, he was so impressed with the young Virginian that he adopted him into his Seneca tribe. He gave him the name *Conotocarious,* which means "Devourer of Villages." George was very flattered because his great-grandfather had acquired the same name during his skirmishes with the Native Americans during the 17th century.

George returned safely from his mission but was unable to bring Governor Dinwiddie any good news.

GEORGE WASHINGTON

"The French would not heed the warning," he told him. "They and their Indian allies are preparing for war to capture the Ohio Valley. We shall have to fight."

Governor Dinwiddie praised George for having volunteered and undertaken the dangerous journey. He promoted him to the rank of lieutenant colonel, put several hundred soldiers under his command, and sent him back to the wilderness to defend the American settlers and their families from French and Indian attacks.

It was 1754 when twenty-two-year-old George Washington, fearless as ever, led the troops from colonial Virginia into the Ohio wilderness. His first engagement with the enemy resulted in an easy victory. The Indian scouts that he had recruited spotted a patrol of sleeping French soldiers. Washington ordered his soldiers quietly to surround the group, and he strode into the clearing and called for the

The Survivors Surrendered to Young George.

enemy to surrender.

Arising hastily, the French fired a hail of bullets at the Virginians, who quickly returned the fire. In less than fifteen minutes the encounter ended. Of the thirty-two Frenchmen, ten lay dead, and the survivors surrendered to young George Washington.

Flushed with this early victory, Washington jotted down a note to be delivered to Governor Dinwiddie upon his return.

If the whole detachment of the French behave with no more resolution than this chosen party did, he wrote, *I flatter myself that we shall have no great trouble in driving them to Montreal.* Before long Washington realized, however, that forcing the French back toward Canada would be a much more difficult task than he had imagined.

Washington and his men built a stockade, which they named Fort Necessity, in a meadow surrounded by high mountains. Washington intended to follow British military strategy by engaging the French and Indians in combat on the open field. But the enemy opened fire from the mountains and forced Washington and his soldiers to abandon the fort and fight in the open field. There they were sitting ducks for trained French marksmen who fired from hiding places in the thick forest.

To make matters still worse, a rainstorm soaked the Virginians' gunpowder, ruined the operating mechanisms on their guns, and left the troops standing waist-deep in muddy water. When the fighting ended, almost one-third of Washington's 284-man force were dead or wounded.

At midnight, Washington and the French commander sat down together. The Frenchman promised not to attack the survivors if Washington agreed to their immediate retreat back to Virginia. Washington hated the thought of defeat and surrender, but he had no choice but to accept the

The Enemy Opened Fire.

French offer. His men had few functioning weapons, and morale was terrible. With a feeling of deep discouragement, Washington and his battered forces straggled home, carrying the wounded on their backs.

For weeks after this devastating defeat, Washington was in a black mood. He lashed out at anyone who dared to criticize his performance. But he had to cheer up for the sake of the men under his leadership.

"Do not despair," Washington told his troops. "We shall return to the battlefield and do better. The king of England is sending one of his best commanders, Major General Edward Braddock, and thirteen hundred troops to help us defeat the French and Indians. If only I can convince the general that a new type of strategy is necessary!"

General Braddock offered George Washington the position of aide-de-camp, a sort of special assistant.

But on the eve of their departure, Mary Washington arrived. She was in a very emotional state.

"Why must you risk your life again in a military adventure?" she demanded, half in anger, half in fear. "Haven't you done enough already?"

"Really, Mother! Have you no faith that God will protect me?"

"Never mind that!" she snapped. "Who'll take care of Ferry Farm while you're gone?"

"I'm quite sure that you can keep the slaves and servants in order," he replied with a grin. Indeed, no one on the farm would dare cross this formidable mistress.

No sooner did Washington arrive with General Braddock's forces on the frontier than his mother sent him an urgent message.

I really must have someone—a Dutchman, perhaps—to manage this farm, she wrote. *And please fetch me a tub of butter at once!*

He Would Not Heed Washington's Warning.

GEORGE WASHINGTON

Honored Madam, George wrote back in a sarcastic letter, *I do hope you realize that I am far from civilization and find it impossible to fulfill your requests. Sincerely, your son.*

General Braddock proved almost as hard to deal with as Washington's mother. He would not heed Washington's warning to conceal his men in well-protected hiding places rather than deploy them in full sight of the enemy.

"You will endanger all of our lives if you don't adjust your battle plan," Washington declared.

"What right have you, a young man who hasn't even grown a beard, to give me lectures?" the general shouted back.

Indeed, General Braddock could not explain to himself why he tolerated Washington's advice. Perhaps he admired him for his pluck and courage, lack of a beard notwithstanding. The general readily disciplined any of his men who got out of line, but his attitude toward Washington was different. Nevertheless, he drew the line at accepting changes to his military strategy.

In preparation for the battle, the British Redcoats (so called because of the color of their uniforms) marched in a straight line onto the field where they were painfully vulnerable to the French and Indian fighters hiding in the dense forest.

"Tell your men to spread out and hide," Washington urged General Braddock yet again. "The way they're marching now, they're easy targets for the enemy."

"I know what I'm doing!" the general snapped in reply.

Sure enough, the French and Indians staged an ambush that killed hundreds of Braddock's troops. "This is the fault of the American colonial leaders! They didn't give us enough supplies and provisions!" General Braddock cursed. These were his last

A Straight Line of Redcoats

words, for the next moment he fell, mortally wounded from an enemy bullet. His army began to retreat in total disorder.

They ran like sheep being chased by wolves, Washington later wrote in his journal.

Washington, in his typical manner, took charge, trying to rally the panic-stricken troops while dodging bullets. Two horses were shot out from under him, and four bullets passed through his battle jacket. Fortunately, he was not injured.

This experience proved to be a signifcant moment in George Washington's life. His admiration for England's military prowess suddenly disappeared. Dressed in his blue uniform and cocked blue hat, Washington felt completely separate and distinct from the English Redcoats. He felt, instead, like an American! Perhaps at this moment, George Washington saw for the first time the necessity of liberating the American colonies from their English motherland. Before this, George and all the people he knew considered themselves loyal citizens of the British crown. The laws they followed were British laws, and the British army provided them with their protection.

But although they dressed and thought and spoke like Englishmen, the colonists were different. Their rich, unexplored land was a very different place than was old England, which George and many other colonists had never even seen. How soon would the differences outweigh the similarities, and which would finally win out?

Americans were just starting to ask questions like these, and no one would play a greater part in providing the ultimate answer than young George Washington himself.

His Small Militia Alone

Chapter 5

George's First Command

The war against the French and the Indians was coming close to the borders of Virginia. Refusing to provide further assistance to George Washington's forces after the defeat of General Braddock, the Redcoats moved the rest of their troops north to Philadelphia. That left Washington and his small band of militiamen alone to defend the Virginia frontier.

It seemed like an impossible task. The French troops were well equipped with guns, and the Indians had long knives. They paraded along the 350-mile-long border of Virginia with belts full of the scalps of defenseless colonists.

George Washington received a frantic letter from the office of the Royal Governor of Virginia.

We must fight and defeat the French and their Indian allies before they conquer Virginia! the letter said. *You are the only man with the skill and courage to command a force against our wicked enemies. And now you also have the battlefield experience. Will you agree to serve?*

Washington, still only 24 years old, was flattered, but he was also cautious. *I don't wish to be considered a mere volunteer,* he thought to himself. *I am a professional soldier now. In order to secure a victory over the enemy, I must have enough troops, equipment, and authority.*

While he was mulling over these thoughts, more letters arrived, begging him to serve. They came not

"You Are the Only Man . . ."

only from the governor's office, but also from other important men in the House of Burgesses, Virginia's assembly.

With all due respect, George Washington wrote, *I cannot serve unless I have a realistic chance to win. Therefore, I will need 40,000 pounds, the authorization to raise a one thousand-man army, promotion to the rank of full colonel, and the position of commander-in-chief.*

Washington received an immediate reply to his message.

All your requests are granted! it said.

As she had so often in the past, Mary Washington stepped in to try to disrupt her son's plans.

"Have you still not had enough fighting?" she asked. "I'm quite sure someone else can be found!"

Washington's answer was short:

"Please remember, dear mother, that I did not seek this assignment. I was asked to serve, and it would be dishonorable for me to refuse. You should be more concerned about my honor than about my going."

Shortly after, George had an encounter with a politician named William Payne. It was election time in the town of Alexandria, and Payne was running for the House of Burgesses against one of Washington's friends. Passing Payne in the street, Washington made a crude remark. Payne responded in similar fashion. Tempers flared, and Payne, who stood barely as high as Washington's shoulder, struck the commander-in-chief of the Virginia army with a hickory stick and knocked him flat on his back on the pavement. Bystanders rushed to assist Washington, but he got on his feet and walked away.

The next morning, Payne received a message from Washington, requesting a meeting in a nearby tavern. The news traveled quickly, and a large crowd gathered at the meeting place, expecting to

Washington Sat Alone at a Table.

witness a duel. The usual procedure in such cases was that the wronged party—in this case, Washington—demanded an apology from his tormentor, failing which he would start a duel to avenge his honor.

This time the spectators were disappointed. There were no dueling pistols in sight. Instead, Colonel Washington sat alone at a table, with a bottle of wine and two glasses in front of him. When Payne approached the table, Washington rose and held out his hand. He completely towered over the little politician.

"Mr. Payne, I believe that I made a mistake by insulting you yesterday. I hope you will accept my hand and sit down for a drink with me. Let us be friends."

Immediately, Payne was transformed from an opponent to a firm supporter of George Washington. Their friendship lasted a lifetime. Payne's family and his descendants, astonished by Washington's actions, never tired of retelling the tale.

The incident with Payne reflected Washington's maturity. He had grown into a self-confident man with firm control over his actions and emotions. He would need every ounce of this hard-won maturity when he returned to the savage war on the frontier.

Although Governor Dinwiddie and the House of Burgesses had allotted money for soldiers and equipment for Washington's army, Washington himself had to obtain them. His attempts to recruit men were a nightmare.

Far from agreeing to fight alongside him or to provide horses, wagons, or provisions for the army that was defending their homes and families, the frontier settlers cursed the army and even threatened the lives of Washington and his officers.

Even the men who reluctantly agreed to join often did not obey orders. Washington tried to discipline them, but they spent much of their time drinking

A Self-Confident Man

wine, stealing, and shirking their duties.

"I simply can't understand this behavior!" Washington complained to his officers. "Instead of fighting to protect their property, their wives, and their children, these recruits desert the army at the first opportunity. The situation is truly frightening. Every day, the French and the Indians set fire to farmhouses. So many innocent people have been captured and killed. When will all this misery end?"

Washington's supporters in Virginia wrote encouraging messages, urging him to keep up the good fight. Beverly Robinson, the Speaker of the Virginia House of Burgesses, writing on behalf of many of the delegates, said, "We have faith in you and are counting on you to bring this war to a happy conclusion."

Washington's opponents appeared to outnumber his supporters, however. Even Governor Dinwiddie turned against him. He threatened to open an investigation into charges of drunkenness, desertion, and immoral behavior among Washington's officers and troops. Washington, in turn, wrote letter after letter to the leaders of the colony, blaming them in part for his lack of battlefield successes. Despite his overall maturity and cool approach to problem-solving, Washington remained extraordinarily sensitive to criticism.

For three long years, Washington's Virginia army fended off French and Indian attacks and tried to protect the settlers and their families in the Ohio Valley. Washington's forces numbered 700 men— two for every mile of frontier. It wasn't enough to cope with wave after wave of attacks.

But Washington began to win the struggle against his troops' lack of discipline. He imposed drastic forms of punishment for such crimes as desertion. Once, for example, a sergeant and the men under his command deserted one of Washing-

Washington Court-Martialed the Sergeant.

ton's officers, who was then killed and scalped by warring Indians.

Washington court-martialed the sergeant and condemned him to death. He requested the Virginia Assembly to give him the authority to carry out the sentence. The Assembly did so. Shortly afterward, Washington ordered the construction of a gallows forty feet high. Two deserters were hanged.

The war continued. Washington was very frustrated because the region where his army fought was considered less important than the North, which was closer to Canada—the heart of French power in North America. At long last, in November 1758, relief came. English forces led by Brigadier General John Forbes moved southward to join Washington. Together, they drove the enemy away for good. The final outcome led Governor Dinwiddie once more to change his opinion of George Washington.

"You've done an outstanding job, George!" the governor praised the commander-in-chief. "You are a true hero of Virginia!"

"Thank you, sir," Washington replied. "It's been an honor to serve the colony of Virginia. But now I wish to retire from military life."

"You Are a Hero of Virginia!"

Chapter 6

Home at Mount Vernon

Washington returned to Mount Vernon. It was wonderful to be reunited with old friends after years of fighting in the wilderness. But Washington was restless. His life was not yet complete.

"I am almost twenty-seven years old already," he told his friends. "I'm ready to find a wife, settle down, and raise a family."

He contacted his agent in London to order new furniture for Mount Vernon. He also took other steps to beautify the mansion and the surrounding land.

George met Martha Dandridge Custis at a dance attended by the cream of Virginia society. Recently widowed, the twenty-seven-year-old Mrs. Custis was one of the wealthiest young women in the colony. She had two small children, Jacky and Patsy. They lived in a huge mansion, called the White House, which had six chimneys.

Washington was attracted to Martha almost immediately. She was just the type of woman he, and Mount Vernon, needed.

"You're all invited to a wedding!" George announced to his friends. "It will be here at Mount Vernon on January 6, 1759."

Shortly before George and Martha were married, however, George was called upon to wage one more military campaign in the wilderness west of Virginia.

He corresponded briefly with Martha while he

The Wedding Day Was Finally at Hand.

was away, telling her, *We have begun our march for the Ohio. A courier is starting for Williamsburg, and I embrace the opportunity to send a few words to one whose life is now inseparable from mine. Since that happy hour when we made our pledges to each other, my thoughts have been continually going to you.*

At last George returned from his military duties, and the couple's wedding day was finally at hand. George and Martha made a handsome couple at their wedding. George, towering above his bride, wore his full-dress military uniform. Martha's wedding dress was made of white satin, with silver threads. She kept the dress for the rest of her life— along with the white military gloves that her new husband wore when he took her hand in marriage.

Guests came from near and far to celebrate with the new couple. George and Martha were very different. He was tall and slim and serious; she was short, plump and always full of laughter. But they seemed happy together. Martha's children welcomed George as their new father, and he treated them as if they were his own.

The relationship between George and Martha was one of friendship and affection. George needed a wife to help tend Mount Vernon and serve as a hostess at important social functions. Martha needed a husband to help manage her estate and be a father to her young children. Some of their friends regarded the union between George and Martha as mainly a business and a social arrangement that offered both of them many benefits, but in fact they cared deeply about each other.

For the next sixteen years, from 1759 to 1775, George Washington lived a very contented and plea-sure-filled life at Mount Vernon. During the days, he rode on horseback around his family's properties, checking on the condition of the buildings, the crops

For 16 Years, a Contented Life

and the slaves. In the evenings, he and Martha entertained guests. They stayed up late exchanging stories and jokes with their visitors. There were also many parties for the children.

George Washington welcomed both the joys and responsibilities that came with being a parent. Martha's children called him "Papa" and treated him with great affection. He loved to buy them gifts, which he usually ordered all the way from London. His first order included "ten shillings worth of toys, six little books for children beginning to read, one fashionably-dressed baby doll . . . and a box of gingerbread toys and sugar images."

Washington also displayed a fatherly concern for the children's welfare. For example, he strongly supported a suggestion by Jack's tutor to vaccinate the boy against smallpox. Having suffered this terrible disease, Washington wanted Jack to escape its misery. But when the vaccine was first developed to protect against it, people were concerned about its safety.

Knowing how much Martha worried about her children, Washington instructed the tutor to arrange for Jack's vaccination along with the other students at the school. Only when Jack was safely vaccinated did George tell Martha.

In addition to his warm relationship with Martha and his stepchildren, George Washington kept in close touch with his siblings and their families. He never stopped missing Lawrence. He was also very fond of his other half-brother, Austin, to whom he wrote: *The pleasure of your company at Mount Vernon always did and always will give me great satisfaction* and signed the note, *Your most affectionate brother.*

Actually, Washington's favorite brother was Jack. He once described this second of his three younger brothers as "the close companion of my youth and

They Visited Mount Vernon Frequently.

the friend of my mature age." In his will, Washington left Mount Vernon to Jack's son, Bushrod.

The relationship between Washington and his other two brothers—Samuel and Charles—was rather cool. Nevertheless he lent them both money on the many occasions when they needed it. Samuel was constantly in debt, and Charles was undependable for most of his life.

George maintained friendly relations with the other members of his extended family, too. They visited Mount Vernon frequently without waiting for formal invitations, and found warm welcomes. On a typical day, Washington reported in his diary: *I . . . returned home a little after noon and found my brother Austin, his wife, daughter Millie and sons Bushrod and Corbin, along with the wife of the first, and my cousin William Washington with his wife and four children.*

Also most notable was Washington's warm feeling

for his mother-in-law, Mrs. Dandridge. His relationship with his own mother, by contrast, continued to be rocky. He was always a good son, visiting her at Fredericksburg whenever she summoned him, supervising the operation of her plantation, and giving her money whenever she requested it.

Mary Washington remained resentful, however. She wanted more than the performance of duty by her eldest son; she wished to dominate him as she dominated her other four children. She complained about him endlessly.

George Washington's generosity toward his relatives and friends was quite extraordinary, even when one considers the large amount of wealth that he had accumulated. He lent money without pressing for repayment, and he often provided money outright as a gift. To avoid embarrassing many recipients, he transferred money secretly.

In one typical action, Washington wrote to

Mary Washington Remained Resentful.

William Ramsey, for whom he had worked as a surveyor in Alexandria, and asked for permission to send Ramsey's son to college. The boy was very bright and liked to study. Washington provided the money to enable him to attend Jersey College, now known as Princeton University.

No other return is expected or wished for this offer, Washington wrote to William Ramsey, *than that you will accept it with the same freedom and good will with which it is made, and that you may not even consider it in the light of an obligation or mention it as such; for be assured that from me it will never be known.*

Two recipients of Washington's generosity wanted the money to advance their careers in the Royal Army. When Billy Fairfax, the younger brother of George William, bought a commission in the Royal Army, Washington sent him money and wrote that he didn't care if it took seven years to repay. Shortly after, Billy died, fighting alongside the English troops on the Plains of Abraham in the battle that captured Canada from the French.

On still another occasion, Washington fulfilled a request from an artist who had once taught drawing to the staff at Mount Vernon. The man wrote, *I prefer to owe you that favor than to anybody else, being certain of secrecy.*

In his later years, Washington took upon himself the burden of educating and otherwise supporting twenty-two nieces and nephews! At one point, he estimated that he had spent a total of more than $5,000 on two nephews alone—the sons of his brother Samuel. Every Christmas, Washington gave from $250 to $500 to charities as well.

Washington was as quick to show anger as to display generosity. He particularly disliked people who were dishonest and those who wrongfully demanded favors.

"I Am Not Accustomed to Such Vulgar Mail."

GEORGE WASHINGTON

Once, he wrote a very nasty letter to a former officer in the militia who had been thrown out of the army for cowardly behavior in the French and Indian War and who had later dared to demand a share of the lands that the Royal government had given to veterans of that battle. The man had written to Washington, accusing him of cheating him out of the land.

Sir, replied Washington, *your rude letter arrived yesterday. I am not accustomed to receiving such vulgar mail. Even if you were drunk when you wrote it, that is no excuse! In your stupidity, you forgot to look in the public gazette, which would have informed you that you received what you were entitled to. Even if you think you deserved more, did you really believe that I would go out of my way to accommodate you? My only regret is that I ever concerned myself with such a rude and ungrateful fellow as yourself!*

GEORGE WASHINGTON

On another occasion, Washington was riding around his plantation when he heard gunfire from the riverbank. Rushing toward the sound, he saw two dead ducks on the shore and a man crouching in a canoe that was partly hidden by tall reeds. He recognized the poacher at once: a man who had often sneaked onto Washington's property in search of waterfowl and other creatures.

"Stop or I will shoot!" shouted the poacher as Washington approached rapidly. He raised himself up in his canoe and aimed his gun.

"It is *you* who must stop!" replied Washington, ignoring the threat and the weapon. "How many times have I told you to stay off my property?"

His face livid with rage, Washington drove his horse into the water, leaned down to the canoe, and dragged the vessel and its passenger onto dry land. Washington then dismounted and threw himself at the poacher, forcing him to the ground on his knees.

He Leaned Down to the Canoe.

GEORGE WASHINGTON

"This is the last time that you will trespass on my property and go home alive!" Washington thundered, knocking the poacher's gun to the ground and leaving him there.

That was George Washington's reaction to dishonesty, as well as his sense of care and responsibility for his property.

Chapter 7

A Peaceful Life

Such unpleasant episodes barely affected Washington's peaceful existence at Mount Vernon, where he and his friends indulged in round after round of parties and other fun-filled activities. They also spent many enjoyable evenings in Fredericksburg, at George Weedon's Indian Queen Tavern, where men with military backgrounds gathered. They joked, sang loudly, and played cards far into the night.

One of Washington's favorite activities was

Clear Across the River!

"throwing the bar." Throwing the bar, a very popular sport in Washington's time, was similar to modern discus-throwing. Although he was already about forty years old, he outperformed men half his age at this sport. The man who threw the farthest received a prize.

"Let's see if your arm is as strong as it is long," Washington's friends teased on one memorable night. They were standing on the shore of the Rappahannock River. Washington happily accepted the challenge.

He whirled the heavy bar around in his huge hand and threw it at least a dozen yards beyond the best toss of his nearest competitor. According to one story, Washington's bar landed clear across the river!

Washington's favorite sport was foxhunting. It appealed to his love of excitement and danger, and gave him the opportunity to use the courage and skill that had distinguished his military service. During the hunts Washington rode a huge, hot-tempered horse named Blueskin. Like all the other horses in his life, Washington had broken Blueskin himself.

"Keep up with the hounds!" Washington would shout at his huntsmen. Washington himself had no trouble keeping up. He and Blueskin plunged through the woods at breakneck speed, over fences and through dense brush. There were trails cut through the trees around Mount Vernon for foxhunters who were less willing to risk life and limb, but Washington craved the adventure and left the trails for others. His diaries for six typical years—1768 to 1774—indicate that he went foxhunting 155 times, compared with 31 times duck hunting and 5 fishing.

George Washington's recreational activities included not only sports but also cultural events. He

"Keep Up with the Hounds!"

particularly enjoyed the theater. Rarely did he miss an opportunity to attend a play when he was in Williamsburg. Another of his favorite pastimes was dancing. His boundless energy was evident on the dance floor as everywhere else. He held many dances at Mount Vernon and typically danced through the entire night, sending the exhausted musicians home at dawn.

Washington had a lifelong love of horses, but he was also very fond of dogs. His favorite seems to have been a French hound named Old Vulcan. On one occasion, Martha had just baked a large ham to serve at a dinner party. Vulcan seized and ate the ham. Although Martha was both furious at the dog and embarrassed among the guests, George matter-of-factly announced that the dinner party would be a potluck affair, since Vulcan had gobbled up the main course.

People in the Virginia colony eagerly sought invitations to the social events at Mount Vernon. The dinner parties there featured excellent food, as well as the best wine, which Washington ordered in 100-gallon kegs. After dinner the guests exchanged toasts, sampled a great variety of nuts, and talked about the major topics of the day.

In view of his active social life, George Washington needed an extensive and fashionable wardrobe. He had a special agent in London to purchase and ship his clothes. His orders to the agent indicated his taste:

I *must have fashionable garments,* he wrote, *but nothing fancy—and, above all, no lace or embroidery! Plain clothes with a gold or silver button . . . are all I desire.* He spared no expense for his wardrobe, ordering his agent, for example, to obtain *a genteel suit of clothes made of super-fine broadcloth, handsomely chosen.* He was equally particular about the other items that he ordered. When

He Wore Plain Clothes on the Plantation.

his carriage broke down, he instructed an agent in England to replace it with one *in the newest taste, handsome, genteel and light...to be made of the best seasoned wood and by a celebrated workman* and decorated with the Washington coat of arms. He specified that the carriage should be painted green *unless any other color more in fashion and equally long-lasting deserves priority.*

Although he dressed to perfection for formal occasions or when hosting an event, Washington wore plain clothes when he was supervising and administering the affairs of his plantation. On one blazing hot summer day, a visitor to Mount Vernon inquired where he could find "General Washington."

One of the servants pointed the man in the right direction and said: "You will meet, sir, with a gentleman riding alone, in plain drab clothes, a broad-brimmed white hat, a hickory switch in his hand, and carrying an umbrella with a long staff, which is attached to his saddlebow. That person, sir, is General Washington."

During the years at home after military service, Washington put his energies into his properties and his business affairs, assuring, above all, that everything was orderly.

There was much to be done. George rose every morning at four A.M. to handle his correspondence and his accounting books. In addition to supervising the affairs of Mount Vernon, he had to manage Martha's thousands of acres of land and more than $100,000 in cash—a vast sum of money for that time. There were complicated transactions to conduct with the Bank of England, and in those day, communication across the ocean was slow and not very efficient.

George Washington's slaves and servants kept clearing more and more land at Mount Vernon until the plantation was like a small city. There was no

Mount Vernon Was Like a Small City.

need for towns or shops, because everything that Mount Vernon's residents needed was made right there. In one building sat the people who spun yarn for clothing and household goods, in another sat the weavers, and in still another sat the seamstresses who handled all the sewing and mending.

There were also blacksmiths, carpenters and stonemasons. Food from the plantation's gardens and fields, and fish from the Potomac River filled the storehouses at Mount Vernon. Slaves worked very hard on the plantation. George Washington took good care of his slaves. He had the reputation of being one of the more careful and caring of plantation owners.

Washington was much more than a good manager of his property. He had a passion for excellence. He was also very creative, ambitious, and imaginative in pursuing his activities. His expertise in business and agriculture was hailed throughout

Virginia. From England he ordered the latest books on agricultural science, which he used as a guide to modernize farming operations at Mount Vernon.

Virginia's standard cash crop was tobacco. Grains, like wheat and corn, were grown mainly to feed the people living on the farm or plantation. Washington decided to raise wheat as a cash crop. He created wheatfields at Mount Vernon and even built a mill. Before long, the wheat was selling briskly on the Virginia market.

Washington also raised corn and rye, partly for use in making whiskey. He even opened a distillery at Mount Vernon to produce the whiskey. In addition, Washington established fisheries on the banks of the Potomac alongside Mount Vernon and caught thousands of pounds of herring, shad and other fish.

Washington even experimented with raising various kinds of animals. Like everyone else in Virginia, he raised horses. But he also determined that

His Breeding of Mules

a good profit could be made from sheep. This idea was entirely original, and it worked. So did his breeding of mules, and they turned out to be cheaper and better farm animals than horses.

George Washington's responsibilities as a property manager were awesome, but so were his talents. He had an enormous amount of energy. He successfully supervised more than 300 workers at Mount Vernon and as many as 600 on the Custis lands.

George was strict but fair with his paid employees. He insisted on periodic written reports about every job performed on his or Martha's lands, whether it be building a fence or surveying the livestock. He required reports be accurate and on time. He refused to tolerate sloppy work habits. In short, he demanded as much from others as he did from himself—and that was a great deal indeed.

In everything he undertook, Washington sought

perfection. He placed a very high value on quality and efficiency, as a note to one of his plantation managers shows:

My goal is to work for profit and therefore to put a premium on quality rather than mere quantity. ... There is no difference between the amount of work required to tend an excellent enterprise and an ordinary one.

Washington's efforts paid off well. He had a good start with both the land that he inherited from his father and brother, and the assets that Martha brought to their marriage. His skillful management then greatly increased the value of all these resources. By the time of Washington's death, Mount Vernon had grown to cover 9,000 acres of land—13 square miles. He owned a grand total of 23,000 acres and estimated his personal wealth at half a million dollars.

According to his heirs, the true value was more

The Difference Between Ordinary and Excellent

than a million. Thus, although George Washington spent many years away from home—either in military service or in public office—he succeeded in accumulating a huge fortune. Martha's son, Jack Custis, became one of the richest men in Virginia, thanks to his stepfather's guidance in managing his assets.

Patsy Custis never grew up to enjoy her inheritance. She developed epilepsy, a disease characterized by uncontrollable seizures. In 1773, at the age of sixteen, she died. George was deeply saddened, but Martha's grief was even greater. As her husband wrote in a note to her relatives, *This sudden and unexpected blow...has almost reduced my poor wife to the lowest ebb of misery.*

After Patsy's death, Martha clung to Jack, her only remaining child, for comfort. She had always been very anxious about her children and tried to protect them in much the same way as Washington's own mother had fussed over him. Martha, however, was good-natured and easy to get along with—in sharp contrast with Mary Washington.

George, who had a great fondness for children, was especially eager to give Jack Custis a proper upbringing. This included, in George's mind, the kind of good education that he himself had missed.

I am determined to make Jack fit for more useful purposes than horse racing, George wrote to his stepson's tutor. But neither Jack nor Martha proved supportive of George's efforts. When Jack turned fourteen, his stepfather noted with sadness that *his mind is . . . more turned to dogs, horses, and guns, indeed upon dress and equipage.*

Jack's tutor agreed, and not long afterward reported, in addition, that the boy had "a propensity for the fair sex." Jack proposed to a lovely woman named Nellie Calvert without even telling his mother and stepfather in advance.

Martha Was Devastated.

GEORGE WASHINGTON

George Washington was quite distressed by this development.

"I'm not asking you to break your engagement," he told the young couple, "but at least wait until Jack finishes his education before you get married."

He enrolled Jack in Kings College, later named Columbia University, in New York, for a two-year course of study. No sooner had Jack entered college when Patsy died. Martha was devastated. During her first marriage, she had lost two other children.

"Jack is my only living child now," cried Martha. "I cannot bear for him to be so far away! Let him leave New York and come back home!"

Washington could not change her mind, so Jack returned to Virginia, and married Nellie. George Washington held no bitterness toward his stepson. In fact, he assured the newlyweds that they were always welcome at Mount Vernon.

In addition to caring for his family and his land,

GEORGE WASHINGTON

George Washington served dutifully in Virginia's House of Burgesses. He was first elected shortly before his marriage and took his seat on his twenty-seventh birthday. A few days later, a fellow delegate offered the following resolution: *That the thanks of the House be given to George Washington, Esquire, late Colonel of the First Virginia Regiment, for his faithful services to His Majesty and this colony and for his brave and steady behavior from the first encroachments and hostilities of the French and their Indians to his resignation after the happy reduction of Fort Duquesne.*

Fort Duquesne was the last French stronghold in the Ohio region where Washington's army fought. Washington stood up to express thanks for the resolution but blushed, stammered, and found himself entirely speechless.

"Please sit down, Mr. Washington," said the speaker of the house. "You clearly are as modest as

Washington Stood Up to Express His Thanks.

you are courageous. Welcome to our Assembly!"

For fifteen years, George Washington faithfully attended the meetings of the House of Burgesses. These were the great years of colonial government in Virginia. Washington sat in the company of Thomas Jefferson, Patrick Henry and other famous men, all highly qualified to debate the important political issues of the day. Unlike the others, however, Washington could not make great speeches. He spoke infrequently and only about the question at hand, not broad statements of political philosophy. In both his public and private life, George Washington displayed great self-discipline and self-control.

Although Washington had more than enough to keep him occupied in Virginia, he could not stop thinking about the vast lands west of the colony. In the House of Burgesses, he helped pass laws that let the men of his old military regiment get acres in exchange for their service in the French and Indian

Wars.

Washington himself bought up the acres of those who chose not to move West. He regarded the western lands as much more than personal property, however. He wrote that *the western country is a spacious haven for the poor and persecuted people of the earth.*

Thus, Washington foresaw the period when people from overseas would come to America to settle. This period indeed came to pass. Large waves of immigrants from Europe and elsewhere, saw America, as Washington himself did, as the great land of opportunity.

In 1769, Washington took a seven-week journey west to determine the value of land there. He was accompanied by Dr. James Craik, who had served as the surgeon of the Virginia regiment and remained one of Washington's closest friends.

Once, the two men met an Indian chief who had

"He Will Never Die in Battle."

fought with the French against Washington's forces. The chief immediately recognized Washington and recounted an episode from the time of the battle: *I called to my young men and said, "Mark yon tall and daring warrior." Our rifles were aimed and they had never missed before, but it was all in vain this time. A mighty power protected him from harm. He will never die in battle. Instead, a great spirit guides that warrior. He will become the chief of nations and the founder of a powerful empire.*

Dr. Craik was shaken by the Indian chief's words and repeated them on many occasions in the following years. Washington, by contrast, dismissed them as mere flattery. He laughed at the thought that he, a colonel from Virginia who had not even succeeded in obtaining a Royal commission for the army, would one day lead a nation and an empire.

Nevertheless, the rapidly worsening relations between England and its American colonies were already creating a situation in which George Washington would achieve everlasting fame.

Little could George himself begin to guess at the future that lay before him. Nor could anyone see the future nation—the United States of America—in the sprawling forests and unexplored lands which both surrounded and stretched beyond the weak, separate, and little-connected colonies that England still thought of as belonging to the mighty British empire forever.

Everlasting Fame

Chapter 8

Commander-in-Chief

Washington's peaceful life at Mount Vernon was interrupted by the momentous political events in American colonial life that led to the American Revolution. Many serious disagreements had arisen between faraway England and the colonies. As the Americans sought more freedom and self-government, men like George Washington, who had natural leadership abilities, were pushed to the forefront of political activity.

By 1763, the Redcoats had taken control of

almost all of North America. The nine-year campaign had cost a great deal of money, and England taxed its American colonies to help pay off the war debts.

"No taxation without representation!" the colonists thundered. This became one of the most popular slogans of the American Revolution. It was a protest against paying taxes to a foreign country, especially because representatives of the colonies were not permitted to vote on issues or to help shape the very laws by which the English ruled them.

While Patrick Henry and other colonial leaders protested the taxes by making angry speeches, Washington took action. Going around Virginia, he personally persuaded about one thousand colonists to sign a pledge not to import any item from England on which the English Parliament had placed a tax.

In response to these rising protests, the British

The Boston Tea Party

canceled all the taxes except the one on tea. They regarded this as a symbol of their continuing control over the colonies. The colonists expressed their outrage in the event known as the Boston Tea Party.

Late one night in December 1773, a group of colonists in Boston, disguised as Mohawk Indians, climbed aboard three British cargo ships and tossed 350 boxes of tea into the harbor. As punishment for this act, England closed the port of Boston, dispatched troops to seize control of the city, and took harsh measures against other American colonies. This harsh reaction fed the fires of the American Revolution.

The Royal Governor disbanded the Virginia Assembly when it attempted to pass a resolution in support of the Boston colonists. In response, twenty-five Burgesses, including George Washington, met privately and decided to call a meeting of the Assembly independently of the Governor. Hearing about this, George William Fairfax wrote to Washington to express concern.

I remain firmly opposed to violence to resolve this dispute, he stated in his letter.

I share your concern, replied Washington, *but I see no hope for a peaceful solution. We have addressed the English Parliament and received no satisfaction.*

Washington had never before allowed a political dispute or other difference of opinion destroy a friendship, but this time his mind was set. On August 1, 1774 in Williamsburg, he announced at a meeting of the Virginia Assembly that "I am ready to raise one thousand men, provide for their needs at my own expense, and march at their head to Boston."

He was one of seven Virginians chosen to represent the colony in the First Continental Congress, which assembled in Philadelphia in 1774. Washing-

"I Am Ready to March to Boston."

ton was in the company of some of the best public speakers in colonial America. While other delegates made long-winded pronouncements and engaged in noisy debates, this giant-sized man observed the proceedings in almost total silence.

During the nightly strategy sessions that followed each day's public statements, Washington played a key role. He exercised remarkable influence on his colleagues.

Patrick Henry himself regarded Washington as the greatest man in the Congress. Of Washington, Henry said, "If the criterion for greatness is an eloquent speech, other men must be cited. George Washington doesn't pretend to be an eloquent speaker, but he has better judgment and more solid information on the events of our time than does any other man in the Congress."

The delegates to the First Continental Congress expressed their determination to stand and fight together against English rule. The Second Continental Congress, to which Washington was also elected, adopted the same position. On April 9, 1775, before the second Congress met, a clash between American militiamen and English soldiers erupted at Lexington and Concord, in the colony of Massachusetts. This was the first bloodshed, the spark that ignited the American Revolution.

"The time has now definitely come to raise an army to defend the colonies against British power!" declared the American revolutionaries. "But who shall lead us?"

The name raised most often was that of George Washington. He was regarded as the wisest and the bravest soldier in colonial America. Washington arrived at the opening session of the Second Continental Congress dressed in the blue and tan uniform of the Virginia militia. He restated his willingness and ability to lead an army against

Commander-in-Chief of the Continental Army

British-occupied Boston.

But representatives of the New England colonies opposed a Southerner for the command of an army whose first task was to free their own Northern territory from the Redcoats.

Despite the objections of some New Englanders, Washington was appointed Commander-in-Chief of the Continental Army, a position that he held for eight years. Washington's acceptance speech was typically short and to the point, but was not entirely lacking in eloquence: "Thank you, gentlemen. I am greatly honored for the trust that you have placed in me. I am especially honored to carry a title that is bestowed by a free people rather than by the head of a foreign power." He also spoke about times past, when members of his family had to purchase commissions in the Royal army.

"My only concern," Washington continued, "is that my abilities and military experience may not be sufficient to enable me to successfully carry out the task that you have given me. I declare, however, that I shall use every bit of the power in me to support the glorious cause of American independence!"

Lawrence would be so proud of me now! George thought, fighting back the tears that welled up in his eyes. *And I wish so much that he were here to advise me. I have never commanded any unit larger than a regiment. Yet, here I am, preparing to challenge the most powerful empire in the world!*

Washington refused to accept any salary for his new position, which was by far the most challenging and difficult of any mission he had ever undertaken. He asked that Congress only repay him for his expenses.

Washington now faced a major turning point in his life. Having spent many years in the comfort of his home and his family, he was about to return to military life. Compared with his new assignment,

Challenging the Most Powerful Empire!

the war against the French and Indians on the western frontier was easy. This time Washington would have to defeat the feared Redcoats, the strongest army in the world!

The fact that he had once fought on their side gave him some understanding of their military strategy and tactics. But, above all, he had some mixed feelings about going sword-to-sword against his former allies. *I could be accused of treason—of betraying my country!* Washington thought to himself as he prepared to commit the ultimate act of disloyalty to the English king.

An undertaking against the "mother country," England, was a tremendous decision. But the American colonies, represented by their delegates in the Continental Congress, were determined to fight and win. And if anyone could bring them victory, it was the brilliant and courageous George Washington.

After dutifully accepting the leadership of the

colonial army, Washington's thoughts turned to his family. He first wrote to his wife, for whom the separation would be most difficult.

My dear Patsy, he wrote, using his affectionate nickname for Martha, *please believe me when I assure you that I did not seek this assignment. On the contrary, I did everything in my power to avoid it. Not only am I unhappy about leaving you behind, but I also fear that I may not have the ability to perform successfully. Nevertheless, it would have been utterly impossible for me to refuse the position without bringing dishonor upon my name and pain to my friends.*

Washington also wrote to his favorite brother, Jack:

I must now bid farewell to the comforts of home for a long while. I am about to embark on a dangerous mission, and I do not know the time or place of its ending. It is like setting sail on a vast ocean in

Washington Rode North.

which there is no safe port. All I ask is that you visit Martha often during my absence. Your company will ease her pain and loneliness.

His feelings for Martha had grown increasingly over the years. They were reflected in the brief note that he sent her from his army post on the eve of the war:

I maintain a deep affection for you that neither time nor distance will change.

With those words, George Washington, the 43-year-old Virginia gentleman, rode north to take command of the colonial army outside British-occupied Boston. It was June 17, 1775.

Chapter 9

The American
Revolution

During the journey, a messenger brought Washington news of a major battle between the British Redcoats and the New England militia. This was the Battle of Breed's Hill—often called Bunker Hill by mistake—outside Boston. The Redcoats won, but failed to stop the siege of Boston that had been mounted by the New Englanders.

When Washington arrived at his command post near Boston, he found the morale of the New Eng-

News of a Major Battle

GEORGE WASHINGTON

lander militia to be high since their excellent performance at the Battle of Breed's Hill. This situation
added to the resentment between the Northern and
Southern colonies that had risen when George
Washington, a Virginian, was chosen as commander
of the Continental Army.

Despite the presence of some brave men among
its ranks, the army that awaited George Washington's leadership was not an impressive force. Most
of the men were untrained volunteers—farmers and
hunters—who had no military experience. Before
long they missed their families and their farms, and
often returned home without telling their officers
they were leaving. Discipline was terrible. Far from
acting as a single unit with team spirit, the troops
behaved as individuals.

Not only was there friction between Northerners
and Southerners—even soldiers from the same
region seemed to dislike each other. Each New Eng-

land colony, for example, regarded itself as separate and distinct from its neighbors.

Washington wrote in his diary: *Connecticut wants no Massachusetts man in their corps; Massachusetts thinks there is no need for Rhode Island men to serve among them; and New Hampshire says that her valuable and experienced officers should not be dismissed.* Then, the governing bodies of some of the colonies wanted permission for their troops to remain in their home territories.

When he arrived to take command of the army, Washington couldn't even determine how many men were available. Instead of the 20,000 he had anticipated, there turned out to be only 14,000 troops. The supply of weapons and other equipment was similarly far short of what he expected. A member of Washington's staff informed him that someone had miscounted the number of barrels of gunpowder; instead of 485, there were only 38 barrels!

Transforming His Unruly Mob

GEORGE WASHINGTON

"When I heard this bad news, I felt like exploding with rage!" Washington later confided to a friend. "Instead, I controlled my anger and simply remained speechless."

Washington realized that the enormous task at hand—preparing his army to wage war against the British—did not allow time for temper to rule him. Even now he was indeed becoming wiser as his military responsibilities increased.

Washington exercised great patience throughout the period of transforming his unruly mob of men into a trained and disciplined military force. He had to deal with fierce rivalries among the colonies in deciding which men would receive officer's rank.

Recruitment of soldiers was also a major problem. The Virginia Assembly, for one, complained that the colony would go bankrupt if it had to raise and support the 3,000 soldiers that Washington required.

Still another quarrelsome issue was the Continental Congress's insistence on approving officers' commissions and appointments to the senior ranks of the army. Corresponding with Congress on such issues used up valuable time that Washington needed for military strategy. Instead of making the necessary arrangements to fortify New York, plan for an invasion of Canada and be ready to repel attacks by hostile Indians whose activities were backed by British support, Washington had to waste priceless hours with paperwork.

The new Commander-in-chief devoted all his boundless energy into the Revolutionary effort, just as he had with every other task he had ever undertaken in his life. Other colonial leaders, by contrast, seemed to lack a sense of duty to volunteer for military service. Patrick Henry, for example, made fiery speeches against British rule, but quit the army when he was not made a senior officer.

Finally, on March 4, 1776, Washington was ready

Wasting Priceless Hours

to launch an attack against Boston, which was heavily fortified by the British occupation forces. He led 3,000 troops against the 9,000-man British force and succeeded in driving the enemy out of the city.

But the war continued. England sent fresh troops to America, and despite strong resistance from Washington's army, they captured New York.

Washington's troops often didn't have enough guns, uniforms, food, or blankets; but the soldiers were brave and loyal to their leader. They admired Washington for his quick mind and his clever strategies. He knew when to attack and when to retreat.

George Washington was not a so-called "armchair general" who remained safely back in his headquarters and issued orders to the men on the battlefield. He was a hands-on commander, participating fully in all the campaigns. He shared all the hardships of his men, suffering cold and hunger and fatigue along with them. He also praised his troops frequently in order to strengthen their morale.

Despite his best efforts, Washington faced an almost impossible task in recruiting and maintaining a strong army. There simply were not enough qualified officers and men available.

"We need a 50,000-man army in which each man enlists for a long period—preferably three years," Washington advised the Continental Congress.

No! came the reply. A large standing army could result in a military dictatorship, Washington was told. This struggle was for a democratic America, governed by the representatives of the people—not for a country based on the power of the army and the one-man rule of a general.

The year 1776 held a string of military dilemmas for the Americans. Faced with these obstacles, even a courageous leader like George Washington couldn't win battles with an army of raw recruits. The fearful behavior and incompetence of these

Alone on the Battlefield

inexperienced soldiers was almost too much for Washington to bear.

At Kips Bay, New York, for example, two brigades of the Connecticut militia—4,000 men in all—fled at the sight of an advance guard of 100 lightly armed Redcoats. Washington could not control his emotions. He flung his hat on the ground and shouted, "How am I supposed to defend America with men such as these?" As officers and soldiers raced past him in panic, he struck out at them in frustration with a cane whip.

Then Washington, still on his horse, found himself alone on the battlefield, roaring with rage. The Redcoats were barely 100 yards away. They could have seized him in a flash. But they were confused by seeing an unguarded American general, and suspected a trap. Finally, one of Washington's aides approached, grabbed the horse's bridle and escorted the commander to safety.

GEORGE WASHINGTON

This incident showed the intensity that lay not too far beneath Washington's usually calm surface. George Washington was so extraordinarily brave—even reckless—in the face of danger that he could not understand or sympathize with fear and cowardice in other men. Thus, although he usually behaved like a gentleman, the sight of cowards touched a nerve in him. The Indians had recognized this streak of rage in Washington's personality when they gave him the name *Conotocarious*.

Washington struggled throughout his life to curb his own tendency to strike out in anger. He fought to control himself in a manner similar to his struggle to tame the many wild horses he had broken. To an amazing extent, he succeeded. He was motivated by the fact that his goal was greater than himself alone: it was the liberation of America from England, and the colonies' birth as a free nation.

On July 4, 1776, the delegates of the Second Con-

He Could Not Understand Fear.

tinental Congress signed the Declaration of Independence, which stated that the colonies were "free and independent states." This act turned the rebellion of the colonies into a full-scale war. The thirteen colonies became thirteen states. Philadelphia became the capital of the new nation. The Liberty Bell rang out and echoed across America.

Five days after the signing of the Declaration, Washington's 23,000-man army faced a 30,000-strong force in New York Harbor. The British inflicted such heavy losses on Washington's forces that troops were reduced to 7,000. New York City was in flames, and what was left of Washington's army retreated across the Hudson River into New Jersey, with the Redcoats in hot pursuit.

Washington's army continued to decline. The promise of a free America seemed to be fading quickly. The Continental Congress, fearing a British invasion of Philadelphia, fled the new capital in a panic. Forgotten was the Congress's fear of military dictatorship. As 1776 drew to a close, George Washington was given virtual dictatorial powers.

The Congress authorized him to call up troops and wage military campaigns at the times and places of his choosing. This one action saved the country.

Washington divided his remaining forces, putting 4,500 men along the Hudson River to protect New England, and about 2,500 in Philadelphia. Shortly before Christmas in 1776, while a snowstorm raged, this second band of ragged soldiers left Philadelphia under Washington's command and crossed the ice-filled Delaware River. The objective was to launch a surprise attack against Trenton, New Jersey, while hired Hessian troops were asleep in their encampment there. The Hessians, from Germany, fought on England's side in the war.

Washington sent an urgent message to Congress

Washington Issued a Proclamation.

for money to pay spies. Within a few days he recruited John Honeyman, a former British soldier who secretly favored the Americans' cause. Washington had Honeyman act as an American defecting to the Hessians. To cover up Honeyman's true role, Washington issued a proclamation denouncing the defection and offering a reward for Honeyman's arrest. Meanwhile, loyal Americans were told to take the "traitor" alive, because George Washington wanted personally to hang him.

Honeyman, one of the cleverest agents of the war, made friends with the Hessian commander, had confidential talks with him and closely observed every detail of Trenton's defenses. Honeyman—according to plan—"arranged" to be captured by an American patrol. He then passed on to Washington all the valuable information he had gathered.

To keep Honeyman's activities believable, Washington ordered guards to put Honeyman in a cell and prepare for his hanging. Then, given the key to his cell, Honeyman "escaped," returned to the Hessians, and told them that the Americans were badly disorganized and barely capable of fighting.

This clever trick probably spelled the difference between success and failure at Trenton. The Hessians were merrily celebrating Christmas when Washington's forces attacked that night. They captured 900 Hessian prisoners of war, hundreds of weapons and a storehouse of supplies.

Lord Cornwallis, one of England's most distinguished military commanders, rushed with his forces to New Jersey but was outsmarted by Washington. In another brilliant midnight strike, Washington's forces marched twenty miles to Princeton, New Jersey, and destroyed three British regiments. Lord Cornwallis found himself staring at the empty American camp in Trenton!

Washington's legendary fearlessness was dis-

Washington Attacked on Christmas.

playcd once again in the beginning of the Princeton campaign. Washington, telling his soldiers the British were not good marksmen, ordered them to form a line along the entire length of the regiment and open fire. Washington himself sat on his horse between the British and American lines as they exchanged gunfire. It was a miracle that he wasn't killed.

When the British fled, Washington, accompanied by a single aide, pursued them. Though he intended to surround and capture the enemy, his own troops were nowhere in sight!

The battle at Princeton illustrated not only Washington's skill and courage, but also his generous nature. In sharp comparison with the fierce hatreds that marked rival armies in later centuries, Washington felt no personal hate toward the Redcoats.

In fact, he displayed remarkable kindness toward the prisoners and wounded men on the British side.

GEORGE WASHINGTON

At the end of the Princeton campaign, Washington came upon several American soldiers robbing an injured British fighter. He angrily drove the thieves away and ordered an aide to stand guard over the bleeding man until an American doctor arrived.

On another occasion, Washington persuaded the Continental Congress to permit British General John Burgoyne, whom the Americans had taken prisoner at the Battle of Saratoga, to return to England on parole to defend himself against his critics in the British Parliament. Washington wrote Burgoyne a letter of sympathy *"with your feelings as a soldier."* Burgoyne read it to the Parliament, declaring that, although it was written by an enemy, *"it did credit to the human heart."*

The victories at Trenton and Princeton marked an important upward turn for America, but did not end the war. Washington soon withdrew with his army to Morristown, New Jersey, to spend the

Washington Suspected a Spy.

remainder of the winter. He was always on his guard, however. Along the main road, he distributed his men two and three to a house for miles, thus creating an impression that he had a sizable army. In fact, his troop strength was only 4,500, compared with 27,000 Redcoats.

During the stay in Morristown, a person claiming to be a businessman appeared in the American camp and loudly proclaimed his hatred of the English. Washington immediately suspected that the man was a spy. He ordered his aides to prepare figures on the army's strength—figures that were greatly exaggerated. Then he invited the stranger to his headquarters for dinner.

After the meal, an aide, by prearranged signal, called Washington into the next room. Washington left the list of figures, purposely unguarded, on a table.

Sure enough, the spy hurried to read the figures,

which were printed on official paper and saying that there were 12,000 American troops at Morristown.

The next morning, the spy returned to New York to convey his information to General William Howe, the British commander. Howe decided that he dare not attack such a large American army! Washington's troops thus survived to fight another day.

The Spy Returned to General Howe.

Chapter 10

Victory!

George Washington was a warrior, a man on horseback. But he never lost sight of the goal of his military campaigns: a free America. He had written to Bryan Fairfax that *an innate spirit of freedom led me to defy England's overbearing arrogance.* This spirit of freedom led Washington to give up willingly the special powers that Congress had given him.

From the start, he had regarded these special powers as temporary in an emergency situation. As soon as the vote was taken, he wrote to Robert Morris, a major financial supporter of the war: *Instead of thinking myself freed from all civil obligations by this mark of the Congress's confidence in me, I shall constantly bear in mind that as the sword was the last resort for the preservation of our liberties, so it ought to be the first thing laid aside when those liberties are firmly established.*

In fact, when Washington gave up his special powers, America's liberty was by no means assured. The Redcoats invaded Philadelphia in September 1777 and remained in control of the capital for the entire year. Washington's forces defeated 6,000 British troops at Saratoga, New York, on October 17, 1777, but this victory did not loosen the British hold on Philadelphia.

Washington had to take his troops to Valley Forge, eighteen miles north of Philadelphia, to wait out a terrible winter. They hastily constructed log cabins for shelter. More than a dozen men would

The Terrible Winter at Valley Forge

sleep in makeshift bunks in a single room with a fireplace. The troops made good use of their time away from the battlefield by drilling and training extensively.

During the stay at Valley Forge, Washington once again used spies to mislead General Howe about American strength and battle plans. He sent a spy to Howe with an offer to furnish him with secret papers "from Washington's own files." For the next several weeks, Washington carefully composed false figures on his troop strength and wrote memos describing plans to attack Philadelphia and New York. Howe believed everything he read, because all the information was in Washington's own handwriting.

Washington was both leader and companion of the troops during the terrible winter at Valley Forge. When soldiers expressed a desire to go home to escape the severe cold and hunger, he encouraged them to stay, and they remained for his sake. They greatly admired both his physical and moral courage. He inspired them with courage and determination.

Farmers and their families from the area around Valley Forge brought ham, potatoes, butter and whatever other food they could spare for the troops. The Americans also began to receive help from Europe. The Marquis de Lafayette came all the way from France to fight at Washington's side and deliver much-needed financial assistance to the Americans, while General von Steuben came from Germany to help train the colonial army.

The friendship between Washington and Lafayette could best be described as a father-and-son relationship. Washington was then in his late forties, while Lafayette, the child of a powerful family of French noblemen, was only twenty-one. His loyalty to Washington was absolute, and he referred

Lafayette Came from France.

to him as his "adopted father." Perhaps for Washington, the young Lafayette was the son that he and Martha had never had. The Frenchman later named his own son George Washington Lafayette.

Martha Washington also visited Valley Forge. In fact, every winter during the war Mrs. Washington traveled north, braving dirt roads, ice, flooded rivers, bitter cold, and disease to share with her husband the rigors of life in a military camp. She traveled as far as 700 miles round trip.

Perhaps Washington's most unusual visitor at Valley Forge, however, was Bryan Fairfax, who was unquestionably loyal to England. Washington risked his position as Commander-in-Chief by receiving Bryan, but he never went back on a friendship. He offered his long-time friend a safe-conduct pass through the army's lines so that Fairfax could travel to New York.

As things turned out, Fairfax was so annoyed

with the attitude and demands of the British forces in New York that he returned to Virginia and wrote a letter praising Washington's friendship and generosity. The letter remains a fine tribute to the qualities that Washington possessed:

That at a time when your popularity was at the highest and mine at the lowest, and when it is so common for men to resent those whose opinions differ from their own, your show of great kindness has affected me more than any favor I have received. This generosity could not be believed by some in New York because it was so far above the run of common minds.

By the time spring came to Valley Forge, the troops were so well trained that when Washington led them into battle against the Redcoats at Monmouth, New Jersey, the British were forced to retreat. They fled under cover of darkness to escape.

Still the war continued. The Redcoats won a

They Used Invisible Ink.

series of battles, ending with the capture of Charleston, South Carolina, on May 12, 1780, by a British unit under the command of Generals Henry Clinton and Charles Cornwallis. After Charleston fell, Clinton returned to New York, leaving Cornwallis, his second-in-command, in charge of the South.

By this time, George Washington had three separate networks of spies behind the British lines in New York. They even used such devices as "secret writing"; that is, they used special ink that was invisible until a special chemical was spread on top of it.

Washington's clever strategies earned him the nickname "the old fox." What Washington could not win by his army's strength alone, he often won by way of his cleverness and his spies.

In July 1781, General Cornwallis moved the bulk of his forces to Yorktown, Virginia. This set the

GEORGE WASHINGTON

stage for a major turning point in the war.

The Marquis de Lafayette played a major role at this point in the American War of Independence. Having established a close relationship with Washington, Lafayette persuaded France to send troops, ships, and supplies to the revolutionary forces. With French help, Washington was able to increase the size of his army to 17,000 men.

"Here's the battle plan," Washington told his officers. "We'll set up a false camp in New Jersey and send spies to Clinton's forces in New York. The spies will plant rumors that our army is planning to attack New York. Expectation of an attack will keep Clinton's men from leaving the city. Then we can strike Yorktown!"

The plan succeeded brilliantly. On October 9, 1781, Washington lit the first cannon to begin the Battle of Yorktown. The ships of the French fleet formed a line in front of the town so that the Red-

Lafayette Persuaded France to Send Troops.

coats could not escape, and Washington's forces attacked by land. Cornwallis, with his entire army, surrendered in only eight days.

The British, badly shaken by this defeat, agreed to enter into peace talks with the Americans. The war continued for almost two more years, but the outcome was never in doubt after Yorktown. A peace treaty was finally signed on September 3, 1783.

"We would like to part as friends rather than enemies," the British admiral told George Washington before the fleet sailed back to England. "I would be pleased to have you dine with us aboard my ship."

"It would be an honor and a pleasure," Washington replied graciously.

When he arrived, the ship's cannons boomed a salute, the Redcoats bowed, and the admiral greeted him officially as the representative of a free and independent country. After dinner, Washington and the British admiral shook hands and bid each other farewell. Then Washington mounted his horse and rode back to Mount Vernon.

He arrived on Christmas Day. He had been away at war for six years.

"Welcome Home!"

Chapter 11

The First President

"Welcome home!" cried Martha, rushing to greet her husband. By her side were two little grandchildren who had come to live at Mount Vernon.

Before long, friends and relatives began to arrive.

"Thank you for making a free America possible," people told him. George Washington had never been happier.

"Put my horse in the stable for a long rest, and hang my military uniform away," he told the slaves. "I'm ready for a long period of relaxation with my family and friends."

One family member was not there to share the celebration, however. Martha's last living child, Jack Custis, had contracted dysentery during his military service. In those times there was no effective medical treatment for diseases such as dysentery. George Washington was thrown into grief and Martha could not be consoled. The Washingtons soon adopted Jack's children, Nellie and George Washington Parke Custis, and raised them at Mount Vernon.

Shortly after returning from the war, George Washington paid a dutiful visit to his mother. Far from praising his historic achievements, Mary Washington criticized him in her timeworn fashion.

"You haven't been taking care of yourself, George," she whined. "You look so tired! I can't imagine what this war has done to your health!"

She reluctantly agreed to attend a victory dance

A Dutiful Visit to His Mother

in her son's honor and entered the room on his arm. After a few minutes, however, she begged to be excused, saying, "It's high time for old folks to be in bed!"

George Washington was the greatest hero in America. But there wasn't much time to relax. He had to turn his attention from military to peace-time activities. The first order of business was to create a government for the new nation of the United States of America. This task involved coping with the many quarrels and disagreements among the thirteen states and negotiating with a stubborn and outspoken Congress.

Some of the army officers argued that a monarchy, with George Washington as king, was the only sensible form of government, but Washington hastily urged them to "banish those thoughts." His own vision was radically different:

"Now that America has won its freedom, I must

devote myself to ensuring that the country becomes strong and wealthy, yet always democratic. To this task I intend to devote the rest of my life!"

In 1787, Washington presided over a meeting in Philadelphia to draw up a new structure for the American government. The Articles of Confederation, which had provided a basis for governing the new nation since 1781, gave too much power to the individual states and not enough to the federal government.

For example, each state was permitted to issue its own money, which had no value beyond the state's borders. A person traveling from Philadelphia to New York would be unable to purchase anything there with his Pennsylvania currency. Washington strongly criticized this arrangement and called for "an indissoluble union of the states under one Federal head." He played a most important role in getting the new Constitution accepted.

The Overwhelming Choice

GEORGE WASHINGTON

The Constitution, which is still the basic framework of the United States government, solved the problems posed by the Articles of Confederation. It gave the Federal government the power to impose taxes, print money and regulate trade, and carry out other functions that would be binding on all the states. In addition, the Constitution created the three branches of government that we still have today: the executive branch, headed by the president; the legislative branch, represented by the Congress; and the judicial branch, headed by the Supreme Court. A Bill of Rights was also attached to the Constitution.

The Constitution states that the executive branch of government is to be headed by a president. George Washington was the overwhelming choice for this position. On February 4, 1789, he was elected unanimously by the eligible voters (only men who owned property could vote) to serve as the first

GEORGE WASHINGTON

President of the United States of America. He took
the Oath of Office on April 30, 1789 at Federal Hall,
on Wall Street in New York City. John Adams was
named Vice President.

"I must have capable men in my Cabinet to be
able to solve all the problems that we confront," he
announced. "The United States of America has a
huge national debt to pay and an army and navy to
rebuild. As my first Cabinet choices, I wish to
appoint Thomas Jefferson as Secretary of State and
Alexander Hamilton as Secretary of the Treasury. I
also propose that Congress, the legislative branch of
our government, should be made up of representatives who reflect the many differing American views
on major political and other issues."

President Washington wished for a non-partisan
government that allowed different point of views to
be heard. But this type of truce among different fac-
tions was too much to hope for. Despite Washing-

April 30, 1789 at Federal Hall

ton's efforts, two distinct political parties emerged: the Republican (later called the Democratic Party) and the Federalist Party.

Washington attached great importance to the judicial branch of government and sought to create a strong Federal court system. He appointed six judges for the Supreme Court, taking care to select one each from the six most populated states. For the position of Chief Justice, which Washington called "the keystone of our political fabric," he chose John Jay of New York, a man widely known and respected for his honesty.

The three branches of government were officially established as directed by the Constitution. The idea was, and still is, a system of "checks and balances" in order to prevent one branch of government from becoming too powerful and enforcing its will on the other branches. Washington strongly favored such a system because it reflected his belief in and his commitment to democracy, to "secure the blessings of liberty."

George Washington had come a long way from the time when, at the age of twenty-one, he assumed his first official position, that of adjutant. When he took the Oath of Office as President, Washington was almost sixty years old and had gray hair, wrinkles and other signs of age. But his energy, vitality and commitment were as great as ever. And he had far surpassed his beloved brother Lawrence in fame and fortune.

Washington set out on a journey around the new nation to meet and talk with the people. He visited homes, inns and social clubs to find out about the people's views, their hopes and their dreams. He wanted to be responsive to their needs.

He was elected for a second term in 1792 and was sworn into office on March 4, 1793. Washington focused his main efforts on economic progress and

He Warned Against Alliances.

national unity. He warned against alliances with other countries that might bring America into a war that did not serve her interests. This principle was put to the test in 1793, when war broke out between Britain and France.

The war created the greatest international crisis of George Washington's presidency. The political conflicts that the war generated in America almost tore apart the government. Washington's Cabinet members were sharply divided; Thomas Jefferson came out most strongly in favor of France, while Alexander Hamilton called most forcefully for support of England. It required an almost superhuman effort on Washington's part to keep the country neutral between the two warring powers of Europe.

During his term of office, Washington also faced conflicts with the Native Americans in the West, and with Spanish forces in the southeast. In 1794, United States Army troops defeated the tribes of the

Northwest Territory at the battle of Fallen Timbers. The treaty signed after the battle helped bring peace to that region. In 1795 the United States and Spain signed an agreement that regulated trade relations between them and helped to prevent disputes between the United States and the Spanish settlements in the areas of Florida and Louisiana.

President Washington's philosophy on foreign affairs was best summed up in his warning to Americans not to get drawn into "entangling alliances" that would sacrifice American interests to those of other countries. Washington believed that America had neither permanent friends and allies nor permanent enemies, but only permanent interests. The President also wanted to avoid needless involvement in foreign affairs because he wanted to devote America's energies and resources into making America itself a strong and economically healthy country.

Agreement with Spain

GEORGE WASHINGTON

During Washington's presidency a new city was built along the Potomac River, just north of Mount Vernon. It was to be named Washington in his honor. It replaced Philadelphia as the capital of the United States.

President Washington took a salary of $25,000 a year. This amount barely covered his expenses. In order to make ends meet, he was forced to sell more than $60,000 worth of land during his two terms as President. Mount Vernon lost money as well during this time. It was extremely difficult for Washington to supervise the plantation when he wasn't living there. Also the slavery system was very damaging. In 1794 Washington wrote to a friend, *Were it not that I am principled against selling Negroes as you would do cattle in the market, I would not in 12 months be possessed of one as a slave.*

George Washington refused to consider a third term as president. After serving for eight years, he retired to his beloved Mount Vernon in 1797, at the age of sixty-five.

"We have much to do here," he told Martha. "The plantation has not been well-taken care of during our absence."

"Can't we have the slaves work harder?" she asked.

"I hope that in the future, hired workers, rather than slaves, will form the work force of this country. I would like a law passed that will abolish slavery," Washington replied.

Abolition of slavery was a radical idea in George Washington's time. Slavery was a fact of life in 18th-century America, and as a Virginia plantation owner, Washington had more than 300 slaves. Nevertheless, he made a provision in his will for freeing all the slaves at Mount Vernon after Martha's death.

He made a special provision for Bill Lee, the faithful servant who had accompanied him on fox-

A Free Man for the Rest of His Life

hunts and on the Revolutionary War battlefields. Washington's last will and testament stated that Bill Lee, who was now old and crippled, could stay at Mount Vernon as a free man for the rest of his life. He was to receive a cash payment each year in addition to the clothes and other necessities that he had been given as a slave.

George Washington was delighted to retire permanently to his plantation home after an extraordinarily active and lengthy career in public service. He once remarked, "I had rather be at Mount Vernon with a friend or two about me than to be attended at the seat of government by the officers of State and the representatives of every power in Europe."

Far from being a refuge where Washington could enjoy the quiet company of "a friend of two," however, Mount Vernon became a stop for visitors from around the world who wished to catch a glimpse of the famous George Washington. The former president once remarked sadly that his home had become nothing more than a high-class tavern. In 1797 he wrote in his diary, *Mrs. Washington and myself sat down to dinner alone tonight for the first time in 20 years.*

Martha had stood at his side during all the history-making events of his life, supervising the household at Mount Vernon, providing companionship during the difficult war years, and perhaps most important, serving as partner and hostess during his two terms as president. George often presented a stiff and formal appearance, but Martha helped him to relax at public functions, to make friends among the politicians, and generally seem more approachable.

On December 4, 1799, while taking his daily horseback ride to inspect his lands, George Washington fell ill. What appeared to be a cold turned

His Daily Horseback Ride

into pneumonia, and on December 14, at the age of sixty-seven, he died. There was a huge funeral procession in Philadelphia, still the capital. About 10,000 people lined the streets. A large white horse passed by the crowd. It carried Washington's saddle, and his empty boots were placed in its stirrups. The boots were turned backward to symbolize the death of the horse's great master.

"It's all over now," murmured Martha Washington as George was laid to rest in a simple brick tomb. "I shall follow him soon." Three years later, Martha died and was laid to rest beside her husband at their beloved Mount Vernon.

As Commander-in-Chief of the Continental Army and first President of the United States of America, George Washington became one of the most legendary figures in U.S. history. His face is carved in stone on Mount Rushmore, in South Dakota, and his portraits adorn museums throughout America—

indeed, throughout the world. And, most Americans see George Washington's image almost every day— on every one-dollar bill.

One of our nation's most important shrines is the tall white marble spire, the Washington Monument, that rises over the Washinton D.C. skyline. At its base is the inscription that best describes George Washington's place in our history:

"First in war, first in peace, first in the hearts of his countrymen."